The Coming Death &
Future Resurrection of American Higher
Education 1885–2017

Also from Richard Bishirjian from St. Augustine's Press

The Conservative Rebellion

The Coming Death &
Future Resurrection of
American Higher Education
1885–2017

Richard J. Bishirjian

ST. AUGUSTINE'S PRESS
South Bend, Indiana

Library of Congress Cataloging in Publication Data
Library of Congress Control Number: 2017938395

∞ The paper used in this publication meets the minimum requirements
of the American National Standard for Information Sciences –
Permanence of Paper for Printed Materials, ANSI Z39.48-1984.

St. Augustine's Press
www.staugustine.net

Contents

Dedication

With heartfelt thanks, this book is dedicated to

Yorktown University's Trustees who graciously provided advice on issues critical to the University's challenge of the higher education Establishment.

The "Founding Faculty" of Yorktown University who, in the year 2000, accepted an invitation to join the faculty of the first solely Internet-based conservative university dedicated to the reform of American higher education.

The students who enrolled in Yorktown University's courses and degree programs from May 2001 to June 2012.

The many shareholders who financially supported Yorktown University's attempt to challenge the American higher education Establishment

Dr. Lewis G. Pringle, who selflessly served Yorktown University as Chief Academic Officer and developed Yorktown University courses in Marketing and Statistics.

and to
Dr. Wade Shol, Dr. Sheryl Brown, Dr. Debbie Evercloud, the late Dr. Thomas F. Payne, Christopher Evans, Larry Stimson, Michael Foudy, and Jennifer Pointer who helped us attain national accreditation.

Preface

This is an account of how and why American higher education is dying.

As such, it is a tale of the political ability of traditional colleges and universities to block startup, high-technology companies from entering the education marketplace, how they did it, and how higher education as a consequence is on the verge of creative destruction.

This is also the story of how one education entrepreneur challenged a system of higher education in the United States and attempted to found the first, conservative, Internet university and introduce intellectual diversity into a system dominated by the Left in the Social Sciences and Humanities.

That system resisted his efforts and the efforts of conservative faculty and investors in Yorktown University at virtually every step of the way. The primary obstacle Yorktown University faced was the system of academic "accreditation" that has remained essentially unchanged for more than 132 years, from 1885—when "regional" accreditation was founded—to the present day.

I am that education entrepreneur and this is an account of what all those associated with Yorktown University accomplished, and what we learned when we attempted to compete with a corrupt system that benefited university professors and administrators but not the hard-pressed education consumer. Though we used new digital technologies, web browsers, and the Internet to build a low cost university on very little financing, the system of "accreditation" ultimately defeated us and Yorktown University ceased offering courses and degree programs for academic credit in 2012. Undeterred, we then entered the MOOC marketplace with massive, open, online courses and priced each college level MOOC at $29.95. But, that same system of academic

"accreditation," supported by U.S. Department of Education regulations, would not adapt to even newer technologies that have
the potential to lower the cost of the first two years of college to
under $999. In June 2016, Yorktown University Incorporated, hav-
ing fought a difficult battle against an academic "Establishment"
dedicated to preserving its institutional interests, was compelled
to shut down.

Richard J. Bishirjian
Yorktown, Virginia

1. Why American Higher Education is Dying

The American academic Establishment has developed and enjoyed inefficient, impractical, and ultimately harmful self-serving traditions because the United States is a wealthy country and we can and do afford mismanagement, obstruction, incompetence, vice, and barriers to competition maintained by members of the education Cartel. According to the Merriam-Webster Dictionary, a "cartel "is" a group of businesses that agree to fix prices so they all will make more money."

Today, however, education consumers are no longer willing to tolerate high college tuition costs. Their revolt can be expected to unleash the creative destruction that this system desperately needs. Random events may be expected to occur that will trigger this creative destruction (another financial crisis, perhaps) that will overtake the education Cartel and force closure of 40% of existing colleges.

After that experience of death, however, I predict that a resurrection will occur and opportunities for higher education reform will develop that give relief to long-suffering education consumers. Death and resurrection are built into human existence and existing "things," like countries and universities, are also capable of rebirth. But, they usually have to undergo a process of "dying" before they learn their lessons and recoup the best of what was lost. The best of what was "lost" in American higher education is "character education."

Character education: instilling virtue, love for one's fellow man, and appreciation of the nuanced truths of the West were once primary aspects of a college education. An educated person was expected to be of good character, not merely the instrument for mastery of work skills. These important aspects of an education are not measurable in terms of behavior, but they are important aspects of what the Greeks called *paideia* and what we once meant when we spoke of "education."

Aristotle asks in the Nicomachean Ethics, "What is the measure of what is right?" He replies, "The good man."

In life we are guided by good men and women whose judgment we trust and whose qualities of character compel us to rely on them as a standard and measure of what is right and wrong, true and untrue, honorable and dishonorable, just and unjust. Developing such good men and women should be the goal of a college education.

The U.S. Department of Education, an arm of the administrative state that dominates American life, isn't interested in this form of education and thus, from 2001 to 2016, hundreds of opportunities were lost to reform this system. Eight years of President George W. Bush and eight years of President Barack Obama were sixteen years of "lost opportunity" for reform of American higher education.

This is an accounting of the creative destruction of American higher education that is now underway even though most American colleges and universities do not see it coming and the few that do are helpless in the face of a threat to their very survival. But, they should understand that half-reforms won't work; they must reform how American higher education is regulated and accredited. Today the system of higher education in the United States has reached a veritable dead end. Tuition costs are the principal cause that an end is in sight, but what is not taught in college today is why higher education in America is dying.

Let's start with an examination of higher education costs in the United States. The cost of a college education is well beyond what working families can afford and only federal and other loan programs, plus tuition discounts, enable Americans to send their children to college.

Here is a list of tuition, room and board costs, at colleges in Pennsylvania that illustrates the problem.

College	Annual Tuition	Room Board	Four Year Total
Bucknell	$46,902	$62,368	$249,472
Haverford	$46,790	$61,784	$247,136
Franklin & Marshal	$48,414	$60,638	$242,552
Dickinson College	$47,692	$59,664	$238,656
Swarthmore College	$44,368	$57,870	$231,480
Gettysburg	$47,480	$58,820	$235,280
Lehigh-undergraduate	$44,520	$56,770	$227,080
Allegheny	$40,260	$52,449	$209,796
Swarthmore College	$44,368	$57,870	$231,480
Elizabethtown	$39,920	$49,740	$198,960
Juniata	$37,870	$49,340	$197,360
Moravian	$35,991	$42,239	$168,956
Lycoming	$34,016	$44,392	$177,568
St. Vincent	$29,540	$40,517	$162,068
Geneva College	$25,220	$34,680	$138,720
La Roche College	$24,749	$36,573	$146,292
York College	$17,630	$27,500	$110,000
University of Pittsburgh	$16,240	$27,800	$111,200
Grove City	$16,154	$24,956	$99,824
Edinboro University	$9,540	$23,862	$95,448

Real median household income in Pennsylvania in 2013 was $52,007 and discretionary income of families earning $52,007 per annum was $2,075. Unless you are exceptionally talented, it will be very difficult to grow $2,075 a year in discretionary income to pay for four years of college when your child reaches college age.

Even when college costs are discounted, sometimes by as much as 40% at some private institutions, few families in Pennsylvania—or any other state—can afford to send their children to the "better" private colleges without taking on substantial debt.

This chart (below), published by the Center for College Affordability demonstrates the gravity of the problem. "According to the Bureau of Labor Statistics, while the Consumer Price Index for all urban consumers (CPI-U) has risen 179 percent since 1980, college tuition and fees have increased nearly five times more—a staggering 893 percent."

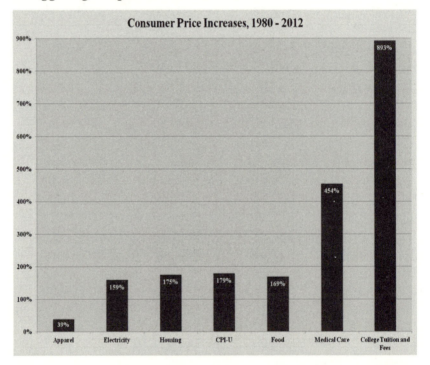

"By comparing the 1980 average seasonal-adjusted annual price for each category to its 2012 counterpart (with a base period of 1982–1984=100), we found that college costs have risen almost twice as much as the increase in the price of medical care, an oft-heralded exemplar of rising costs, and over six times more than the prices of food, housing, electricity, and apparel."[1]

Ignored by the education Establishment and education regulators is a "Get a College Education" hype by high school counselors who push many unprepared students into degree programs for which they must go into debt. Many would be better off choosing a vocational skill and enrolling in a program that leads to employment.

In September 2012, the U.S. Department of Education released three-year default rates for Fiscal Year 2009. Statistics of three-year default rates for Texas colleges indicated that a significant percentage of students in Texas enter college, go into debt to earn a diploma, drop out and default on their student loans.[2]

Here are the three-year default rates from institutions in Texas reported in 2012.[3]

SCHOOL	Borrowers	Default Rate
WESTERN TECHNICAL COLLEGE	2,105	29.10
VALLEY GRANDE INSTITUTE	430	22.19
VERNON COLLEGE	594	22.05
MIDLAND COLLEGE	126	20.93
COLLIN COUNTY COMMUNITY COLLEGE	2,084	20.67
TYLER JUNIOR COLLEGE	3,229	25.33
LAREDO COMMUNITY COLLEGE	472	20.27
TEMPLE COLLEGE	3,705	24.35
LAMAR STATE COLLEGE - ORANGE	491	20.00
MCLENNAN COMMUNITY COLLEGE	3,292	23.12
TRINITY VALLEY COMM. COLLEGE	908	25.00
GRAYSON COUNTY COLLEGE	249	21.49
CEDAR VALLEY COLLEGE	377	24.09
PRAIRIE VIEW A & M	4,587	20.37
CISCO COLLEGE	694	22.06
LEE COLLEGE	515	23.18
MOUNTAIN VIEW COLLEGE	258	22.58
ALVIN COMMUNITY COLLEGE	446	20.11
WILEY COLLEGE	864	27.18

LONE STAR COLLEGE- NORTH HARRIS	2,814	21.30
TEXAS STATE TECH - HARLINGEN	1,151	27.68
BLINN COLLEGE	6,117	20.92
HOUSTON COMMUNITY COLLEGE	5,808	21.89
TEXAS STATE TECHNICAL- MARSHALL	130	32.95
HOUSTON COMMUNITY COLLEGE	5,808	21.89
TEXAS STATE TECHNICAL- MARSHALL	130	32.95
COASTAL BEND COLLEGE	633	28.40
SAN JACINTO COMMUNITY COLLEGE	1,237	20.63
AMARILLO COLLEGE	2,052	22.63
TEXAS STATE TECH-WEST TEXAS	850	26.53
PALO ALTO COLLEGE	437	21.63
RANGER COLLEGE	157	25.00
LON MORRIS COLLEGE	171	29.41
HOWARD COLLEGE	699	24.71
CLARENDON COLLEGE	279	25.81
NAVARRO COLLEGE	2,639	29.27
HILL COLLEGE	668	28.45
SOUTHWEST TEXAS JR COLLEGE	357	23.02
TEXAS SOUTHERN UNIVERSITY	5,360	26.33
TEXAS STATE TECHNICAL COLLEGE	2,330	33.98
KILGORE COLLEGE	1,353	28.91
HUSTON - TILLOTSON UNIVERSITY	607	31.36
JARVIS CHRISTIAN COLLEGE	489	39.57
TEXAS COLLEGE	618	40.90

Student loans in default cannot be erased by bankruptcy and though, for example, Texas residents attending Kilgore College, a two-year institution, pay only $3,360 in annual tuition, 28.91% or 391 of all Kilgore students were reported to be in default on their student loans. After these three-year default rates were published, Kilgore College outsourced "default prevention services" and delinquency rates were reduced to 21.6%. The three-year default rate was lowered by hiring a debt collector, but there is no evidence that Kilgore ceased enrolling students who are not qualified.

Non-dormitory resident, commuting, students at Texas College, a historically black institution, pay $5,000 in annual tuition, but 244 students (40.9%) were in default on student loans. Since a 30% default rate is grounds for loss of access to Title IV subsidized tuition loans and grants, by 2016 Texas College successfully reduced its three-year default rate to 26.1%. Again, debt collecting worked, but there is no evidence that admission standards were raised.

In 2016 the U.S. Department of Education published a list of 3,930 colleges, schools and universities offering college degree programs and the percentage of students who were in default on their student loans.[4] The number of institutions reporting three-year default rates in excess of 24% is astounding and indicates a massive systemic failure in the administration of Title IV loans.

What can and should be done to improve how a college education is financed? Certainly, better screening of applicants for admission and a requirement that marginal students complete remedial coursework is necessary. In most instances, however, students who can't write or do basic mathematics are admitted and are simply passed on from course to course.

It is clear that our education and political leaders have not yet addressed how to remedy a system in which 24% to 25% of students enrolled in a very high percentage of American colleges do not complete a degree program and default on student loans. The message given to every high school student in the United States, "Go to college," is not a solution. In Chapter 15, we outline thirteen actions that can solve this crisis.

Too many elected state officials are uninformed about the realities of their state college and university systems or have allowed themselves to be co-opted by the public universities in their states.[5] Yet, the solution is simple: reform the way colleges and universities are accredited, disconnect accreditation from qualifying for access to Title IV-subsidized student loans and grants, and, above all, direct more high school students into training programs that match their interests and skills, instead of pushing them into college-level programs if they are not prepared to do college-level work.

There isn't much that can be done today for students in default of student loans of $10,000 or even $150,000 or more, but there is hope that new technologies and a consumer revolt against outrageously high college tuition costs will lead to what Schumpeter called "creative destruction."[6]

The high cost of a college education will be lowered by market forces once new entrants into the higher education marketplace are permitted to deliver education products at low cost. But, I am less optimistic that character education will recover and be seen to be the most important outcome of earning a college education. That is the greater challenge facing American higher education, and requires moral leadership seldom found in the administration of our colleges and universities. But, let's first examine the financial crisis that education consumers face.

2. The College Tuition Debt Time-Bomb

More than forty million Americans carry student tuition loan debt. The total amount of tuition debt is estimated to be $1.2 trillion. Students who attended four-year institutions incurred at least $18,000 in student loans and many incurred $29,000 in debt. This Table lists student tuition loan indebtedness at four-year institutions by state:[7]

State	Year		Percent
Alabama – 4-year or above	2013–14	$29,425	54
Alaska – 4-year or above	2013–14	$26,742	50
Arizona – 4-year or above	2013–14	$22,609	57
Arkansas – 4-year or above	2013–14	$25,344	55
California – 4-year or above	2013–14	$21,382	55
Colorado – 4-year or above	2013–14	$25,064	56
Connecticut – 4-year or above	2013–14	$29,750	62
Delaware – 4-year or above	2013–14	$33,808	62
District of Columbia – 4-year or above	2013–14	N/A	N/A
Florida – 4-year or above	2013–14	$24,947	54
Georgia – 4-year or above	2013–14	$26,518	62
Hawaii – 4-year or above	2013–14	$24,554	47
Idaho – 4-year or above	2013–14	$26,091	72
Illinois – 4-year or above	2013–14	$28,984	67
Indiana – 4-year or above	2013–14	$29,222	61
Iowa – 4-year or above	2013–14	$29,732	68
Kansas – 4-year or above	2013–14	$25,521	65
Kentucky – 4-year or above	2013–14	$25,939	64
Louisiana – 4-year or above	2013–14	$23,025	47

Maine – 4-year or above	2013–14	$30,908	68
Maryland – 4-year or above	2013–14	$27,457	58
Massachusetts – 4-year or above	2013–14	$29,391	65
Michigan – 4-year or above	2013–14	$29,450	62
Minnesota – 4-year or above	2013–14	$31,579	70
Mississippi – 4-year or above	2013–14	$26,177	60
Missouri – 4-year or above	2013–14	$25,844	59
Montana – 4-year or above	2013–14	$26,946	67
Nebraska – 4-year or above	2013–14	$26,278	63
Nevada – 4-year or above	2013–14	$20,211	46
New Hampshire – 4-year or above	2013–14	$33,410	76
New Jersey – 4-year or above	2013–14	$28,318	68
New Mexico – 4-year or above	2013–14	$18,969	48
New York – 4-year or above	2013–14	$27,822	61
North Carolina – 4-year or above	2013–14	$25,218	61
North Dakota – 4-year or above	2013–14	N/A	N/A
Ohio – 4-year or above	2013–14	$29,353	67
Oklahoma – 4-year or above	2013–14	$23,430	55
Oregon – 4-year or above	2013–14	$26,106	62
Pennsylvania – 4-year or above	2013–14	$33,264	70
Rhode Island – 4-year or above	2013–14	$31,841	65
South Carolina – 4-year or above	2013–14	$29,163	59
South Dakota – 4-year or above	2013–14	$26,023	69
Tennessee – 4-year or above	2013–14	$25,510	60
Texas – 4-year or above	2013–14	$26,250	59
Utah – 4-year or above	2013–14	$18,921	54
Vermont – 4-year or above	2013–14	$29,060	65
Virginia – 4-year or above	2013–14	$26,432	60
Washington – 4-year or above	2013–14	$24,804	58
West Virginia – 4-year or above	2013–14	$26,854	69
Wisconsin – 4-year or above	2013–14	$28,810	70
Wyoming – 4-year or above	2013–14	$23,708	46

Though the original purpose of Title IV of the Higher Education Act of 1965 was to make a college education available to everyone, college tuition costs have grown as a result of the availability of Title IV loans and grants. But, as discussed in the following pages, an unbending regulatory system is also responsible. U.S. Department of Education regulations governing access to Title IV loans and grants deter advances in technology that make it possible to learn "at a distance." That was not foreseen when the Higher Education Act of 1965 was enacted. We consider the reasons for that in Chapter 7, "Distance vs. Classroom Education."

President Lyndon Johnson chose his alma mater, Texas State University in San Marcos, Texas as the site for signing the Higher Education Act of 1965. When Lyndon Johnson was a student at Texas State, San Marcos was a backwater town. LBJ was sensitive about the education he received relative to the Harvard-educated policy wonks who flocked to work for the administration of his predecessor, John F. Kennedy. His choice of San Marcos, Texas was intended to affirm his commitment to the welfare programs of the New Deal and expressed his desire to snub the East Coast elites who called him "Rufus Cornpone."

The Act was signed into law in November 1965, a year after LBJ's defeat of Sen. Barry Goldwater (R-AZ) in the 1964 Presidential election and established a program that would transform the way American higher education is financed. That financing, and the regulations that govern access to it, would also drive up the cost of a college education to levels that now portend a revolt by education consumers that threatens to destroy how American colleges have operated.

Long before November 1965, Morrell Land Grant Acts beginning in 1862 provided for the creation of Land Grant colleges, by which states were granted 30,000 acres of federal land for each member of Congress in 1860. The states were then permitted to sell the land to finance the creation of agricultural colleges. Nearly all of the land grant colleges are public institutions, and thus the mix of colleges and universities in the United States was given a firm "public"—state owned—boost.

A second formative public program that grew American higher education is known as the "GI Bill." The Servicemen's Readjustment Act of 1944 provided, among other benefits, for cash payments for tuition and living expenses to attend college. Over the next twelve years, 2.2 million veterans used the GI Bill's education benefits.

Student tuition loans were financed by banks who agreed to provide loans that were guaranteed by the federal government. This private sector component allowed private banks to establish banking relations with clients who could expect to use their banking services into adulthood. Opponents contended that "billons" went into the pockets of banks.

In 2010, the Health Care and Education Reconciliation Act made the Federal Direct Loan Program a sole government-backed loan program. The system by which student loans were funded by private lenders, but guaranteed by the federal government, was replaced by a system managed by the federal government. Proponents of this legislation predicted savings of $87 billon over ten years. Today student loans make up 31% of all U.S. assets, thus increasing the political role that student loans play in American politics. Sen. Bernie Sanders, candidate for the Democrat Presidential nomination in 2016, called for free tuition for the first two years of college. Hillary Clinton proposed free tuition at public universities for the first two years for families earning up to $125,000. One must assume that this is mere campaign rhetoric with no chance of becoming public policy. But every private college and university in the United States is at risk, if Congress enacts legislation that provides "free" tuition at public universities and colleges.

Some way must be found to reduce reliance on the Title IV student loan program, and one way to do that is to transfer 5% of annual Title IV funds to the states in Block Grants. As I indicate in Chapter 14, "Fighting the Higher Education Establishment," I proposed that to Republican staff members of the House Education and Workforce Committee. They didn't like that idea, I fear, because they see themselves as guardians of the Higher Education Act of 1965, and anything that challenges or replaces that Act will radically transform what they do for a living.

But, if anything is true in higher education today, business as usual is not working.

3. Why Higher Education Cannot Adapt

Some claim can be made that traditional institutions, looking at new competition, are putting courses online and beginning to expand their delivery of courses from the classroom to the Internet. They are not, however, restructuring how they manage those traditional colleges and universities.

For example, in 2008 executives at the University of Illinois proposed the creation of a parallel for-profit Internet institution that did not report to the traditional departments at the main campus. A faculty meeting was held and the faculty voted it down. In traditional institutions, which are hierarchically administered by powerful interests, decisions are taken in a collaborative process with management hindered by tenured "employees" who are legally a part of management.

On political grounds, nothing, I believe, can be done to effect reform from within under such conditions. But there are also economic reasons.

California had long made college an entitlement for California citizens. But, the state is no longer able to sustain that entitlement. Here is a chart published by California State University showing increases in tuition of more than 46% from 2007 to 2016.[8] Fees increased by 50%.[9]

SYSTEMWIDE AVERAGE – 10 Year Fee History

| FISCAL YEAR/FEE | 06/07 | 07/08 | 08/09 | 09/10 | 10/11 | 2015-16 Fee Rates | | | | |
						11/12	12/13	13/14	14/15	15/16
BASIC TUITION										
Undergraduate	$2,520	$2,772	$3,048	$4,026	$4,440[1]	$5,472	$5,472	$5,472	$5,472	$5,472
Credential Program	$2,922	$3,216	$3,540	$4,674	$5,154[1]	$6,348	$6,348	$6,348	$6,348	$6,348
Graduate/Post Baccalaureate	$3,102	$3,414	$3,756	$4,962	$5,472[1]	$6,738	$6,738	$6,738	$6,738	$6,738

CAMPUS BASED FEES										
Total Campus Based Fees[1]	$678	$749	$802	$866	$938	$1,045	$1,140	$1,214	$1,287	$1,343

Concerned that the California State University system cannot be sustained by taxing California residents, Gov. Jerry Brown attempted to introduce MOOCs in required subjects at San Jose State. MOOCs (massive, open, online courses) permit large numbers of student enrollments in each course which has the potential to lower per-course tuition costs. After a brief first attempt, a mere six MOOCs were offered and priced at $150 per course. But enrollments were capped at between 35 and 150 students![10]

Limiting enrollments is related to the real costs of administering each course at San Jose State.

Out-of-state tuition costs are always a good guide to ascertain what it really costs to administer a three-credit course. The cost per unit for non-residents at San Jose State, except in the Winter 2017 session, is $372 or $1,116 per three-credit course.[11]

Thus the $150 tuition cost of San Jose state's first MOOCs represents about 13% of their actual cost. In other words, San Jose State has decided that it will offer a limited number of MOOCs and subsidize them at a cost of $971 each.

That certainly is not the reason that California Gov. Jerry Brown hoped that low-cost MOOCs could solve his problems in financing the California's state college system.

The American system of higher education developed long before the development of the Internet, and regional accreditation "Standards" require offering courses in classrooms from a physical campus. If it costs between $900 and $1,000 to administer one student in each course that is offered, then the lower costs of disseminating Internet-delivered courses are defeated by the costs of operating a physical campus.

This means that when and if regulations that drive up the cost of tuition change—in order to lower the cost of a college education—every college and university with a fixed campus will be unable to compete with lower-cost Internet education companies.

4. For-Profit Higher Education as "Class Enemy"

While we now have the technologies to lower the cost of the first two years of a college education to under $500 a year, and thus challenge traditional campus-based institutions of higher education with low cost alternatives,[12] the Administrations of Presidents George W. Bush and Barack Obama ignored these technologies and continued governmental policies that oppose innovation.

The "Spellings Commission," discussed in Chapter 14, didn't have the wit to propose the breakup of the education cartel and instead imposed a system of measuring "Learning Outcomes."

Washington education bureaucrats in Republican and Democrat administrations ignored strides made by Capella University, American Public University, Walden University, and the University of Phoenix—all innovative and fast-growing, for-profit, companies with "flat" organization structures.

How do institutions with flat organizational structures operate compared to traditional hierarchical businesses? To answer, we must first become aware that their use of new technologies changes how they conduct their business.

In *The Twilight of Sovereignty*, Walter B. Wriston wrote:

Hierarchical organizations provide tight control of a large group of workers by placing relatively small groups of workers, or submanagers, under the direct supervision of a higher manager. Thus, the steepness of the management pyramid. Flatten that structure and the people within it get a lot less direct supervision. It becomes more important for organizations to have well-understood common goals by which workers can direct themselves. The job of instilling such goals has more to do with persuasion and teaching and leadership than with old-style management. Successful business leaders are finding that the skills of a good political leader are more relevant than those of the general.[13]

Administrators are team members who "operate more like professional workers, who offer their own particular skills to an operation, than like managers, who are defined by their place in the structure."[14]

The use of new technologies by Internet-based, for-profit, education companies promises to take students away from traditional institutions, and as they grow in influence they can be expected to have greater political influence. Again, I quote Wriston: "[T]hey themselves will fight to reduce government power over the corporations for which they work, organizations far more democratic, collegial, and tolerant than distant state bureaucracies inhabited by men and women who never seem to have enough knowledge to temper or justify their power."[15]

So, change will come when those using new technologies have greater political power?

The United States is a country of 330 million-plus people and that's all we can say about the creative destruction that new technologies in higher education can bring?

Resistance to change is endemic to American colleges and universities. Though these institutions are governed by administrators and faculty who are far to the political Left of most Americans, they are very "conservative" in the way they view prospect for change. And since 1965, dependence on U.S. government subsidies of student tuition has led to unparalleled increases in the cost of a college education.

Today American middle-class families are unable to provide a college education for their children without going into extraordinary debt. Many students who were encouraged to go to college, but found that college wasn't for them, default on their student loans. Since bankruptcy does not resolve that indebtedness, their ability to purchase a vehicle, a home, or pay for emergency medical expenses is impaired by that default.

Unfortunately, as discussed in Chapter 11, in 2009, a powerful President of the United States permitted his Deputy Under Secretary of Education, Robert Shireman, to design and put into effect policies that are now destroying the main source of innovation in higher education—for-profit higher education.

How can actions as radical as that be explained? A long history of fascination with socialism took root in the nineteenth century when labor unions were first organized, and gained strength in the twentieth century during the Great Depression. Even though these ideas have been "Americanized," their roots in the socialism of Marx and Engels cannot be ignored.

In good Marxist fashion, for-profit education in the United States has become the designated class enemy of the Obama Administration. The origins of opposition to for-profit enterprises by President Obama have been documented by Dr. Stanley Kurtz in "Radical in Chief. Barack Obama and the Untold Story of American Socialism."[16] This attack on for-profit education is ideological and is embodied in socialist values fostered by American labor unions going back as far as the founding by socialist Eugene Debs of the American Railway Union (ARU) in 1893, and the Industrial Workers of the World (IWW) in 1905. That socialist opposition to for-profit education may be seen in Ohio where White Hat Management, founded by Akron entrepreneur David Brennan, an owner of fifteen Charter schools, has been attacked by the AFL-CIO.[17]

5. Creation of an Education Entrepreneur

My story is that of an education entrepreneur who believes that for-profit education is intellectually and politically acceptable. That story began when I was an undergraduate and I was offended by the moral relativism and liberal politics of my college instructors.[18]

A senior classmate who was active in the college Republicans organized us into a conservative study group and that experience led me to graduate school at the University of Notre Dame where "conservative" European scholars dominated the Department of Government. They had emigrated from Germany, Austria, Russia, Spain, Hungary and Czechoslovakia to escape from Soviet communism, Italian Fascism and German Nazism. There, twenty years after the end of World War II, I was fortunate to study classical political philosophy from Gerhart Niemeyer, Eric Voegelin, Henri Deku and other émigré professors.

A similar intellectual encounter occurred at the University of Chicago where Leo Strauss attracted generations of students who turned against the "value free" political science of the 1960s.

By the time I could seek employment as a college teacher, higher education had long been non-receptive to classical political theorists steeped in Plato and Aristotle, especially if they were political conservatives, for at least half a century. There were some lone "conservative" colleges that held out against the drift to the Left, but not many. I had an interesting, but unsuccessful experience at the University of Dallas.

There I found that a battle royal was being waged in the Politics and Literature Ph.D. program between three conservatives, including Melvin Bradford, Frederick Wilhelmsen, and Thomas

Landess, and faculty influenced by Leo Strauss. I soon became a casualty in a battle for domination of the program and left Dallas to teach at a college in New York founded by the Ursuline religious order.

One advantage of that move was proximity to Manhattan where Neoconservatives had just announced that they were now Republicans. I became friends with Irving Kristol who invited me to some of his events where I met many of his acolytes, Mike Joyce and Les Lenkowsky in particular.

We were on the cusp of the "Reagan Revolution," and books published by Basic Books and Arlington House, and essays published in journals such as Commentary, National Interest, Public Interest, National Review, Modern Age and Human Events were establishing the conservative movement as an intellectual force to be reckoned with in American culture and politics. The college campus where I was an Assistant Professor of Political Science was located about a mile from Arlington House and the Conservative Book Club. When a management shakeup at Arlington House occurred, I became a Senior Editor and recruited conservatives to write for the Conservative Book Club.

John O'Sullivan, at that time, was editor of National Review and he gave me an opportunity to write for NR. I am not a journalist, however, and that didn't work out. But, I became an elected Republican Committeeman from Tarrytown, New York, and invited political pollster, Arthur Finkelstein, whose office in Rye, New York, was a short drive from my college campus, to teach in my Department. I was invited to join a little group of Republicans that Arthur formed. Among that group were Priscilla Buckley and Carol Learsey, Bill Buckley's sisters. Later, when Arthur managed the successful campaign of Alfonse D'Amato for U.S. Senate, Sen. D'Amato hired me to join his staff in the U.S. Senate.

The 1,550 miles from the University of Dallas to New York were actually light years in time from a university controlled by Louise and Donald Cowan, who were intellectual descendants of Southern agrarians[19] and students of the Vanderbilt school of literary criticism. I discovered that these stalwart Southern educators were still reeling from the destruction of Southern culture in the Civil War in the nineteenth century and were uncomfortable living in a city where the assassination of JFK in the twentieth century brought criticism on Dallas as a center of right-wing extremists. The Cowans were uncomfortable with a growing "conservative" movement and were determined to shape their vision of Southern literature upon a university founded by Robert J. Morris, an anti-communist activist. Non-Southerners not steeped in the writings of Faulkner, Caroline Gordon, Andrew Lytle and the Agrarian South of "I'll Take My Stand" found themselves out of place. Because Southern literature is not philosophy or theology, those of us on the faculty who were trained philosophers or theologians, not literary critics, were perceived as "difficult." We were also perceived as alternative sources of authority and thus a potential threat to Louise Cowan's need for absolute subservience.

To my benefit, New York was then, and is now, the center of American commerce, publishing, and intellectual life. New York City may be dominated by Liberals, radicals, poseurs and the arrogant detritus of Leftist movements, but if you want to make a name for yourself, New York City is where that can be done. Due to friendships gained as a young member of the Conservative movement, when Ronald Reagan was elected President, I was invited to join his transition team and later accepted a presidential appointment in his first administration. I never returned to that college in New Rochelle, New York, where I had been teaching and began a career outside academe.

My migration from university employment was common among conservative academics. College teachers are very much on the Left of the political spectrum in America and not very compatible workmates for those who do not share their Liberalism. Most have limited life experience and tend to magnify the importance of their narrow academic turf. They feel threatened by conservative ideas which they imagine are similar to the Nazi movement of Adolph Hitler. Clearly, this is a pathology that cannot be remedied by examination of reality and explains why so many conservative intellectuals must find work outside the ivy walls of American colleges and universities.

The economists who founded the school of Supply-side economics are an example. All were employed outside academe as business consultants, members of congressional staff or staff of congressional committees. Some, like Jack Kemp (R-NY) and William Steiger (R-WI), were members of Congress.

The reasons for lack of presence of conservatives in Academe had a lot to do with the success of the Progressive movement, especially during the Great Depression, when classical liberalism and free market economics were replaced by the economics of John Maynard Keynes and variations of Marxist and socialist economics.

This intellectual disarray in economics expanded into dominance of a theology of the Social Gospel and "Social Justice" that, at private religious colleges and universities, filtered the Gospels through a prism of social action. "Love thy neighbor as thyself," became "Use government to improve your neighbor's lot."[20] The radical transformation of American religious colleges into secular institutions in the twentieth century was a great tragedy that Father James Burtchaell has catalogued in *The Dying of the Light*.[21]

Though I was no longer a practicing academic, I naturally gravitated to university employment and found work at a German state university.

One of the assignments that I was offered in 1987 by Dr. Nikolaus Lobkowicz, president of Katholische Universitat Eichstatt in Bavaria, was to raise private donations for one of his special projects. He thought that massive changes were occurring in Czechoslovakia, Poland, Hungary and other countries in Eastern Europe and desired to help his contacts in those countries to tell their stories to interested persons in the West.

I designed the first, American style, direct-mail fundraising letter for this German state university and visited some German corporate executives who expressed interest, but wanted to learn more. In one memorable meeting with Hans L. Merkle, Managing Partner of the Bosch Corporation, I gained insight into the mind of German industrialists and how they viewed academia in Germany. I learned that when Count Nikolaus was President of the University of Munich, students took possession of university buildings and wouldn't leave. "For the first time since Hitler," Dr. Merkle informed me, "a university president invited the police to restore order on campus." That Count Nikolaus was also a member of an important royal family was important to this gentleman, as was the Bosch name.

Very directly, he asked, how much do you want?

I was not prepared for that question and did not want to request a sum that was unreasonable, so I asked him if he had heard of Groucho Marx. "Yes," he said, "I know Groucho."

I told him that Groucho met with the representative of a cigar company who asked him to endorse his company's cigars and gave him a check for $10,000. "Well, Groucho said, I'm interested, but I've never smoked your cigars." Groucho took a cigar, lit it and said it was a good cigar and accepted the $10,000 offer.

After a couple more puffs, Groucho asked, what would you have done if I said I wouldn't endorse your cigars. The man replied, I would have given you the other check.

Instead of throwing me out of his office, the Managing Director of the Bosch Corporation told me that during World War II, Bosch operations were taken over by occupation forces and an American colonel registered the Bosch name in the United States. After the war, the Bosch Corporation wanted its name back and Managing Director Merkle went to the United States and offered to buy back his company's name for one dollar which he had endorsed in the form of a company check. He said, "You have no right to our company's name."

I was curious to know what the miscreant Army colonel said in reply and I was told, "I gave him the other check."

A large donation to Count Nikolaus followed.

In service to Count Lobkowicz, I traveled in 1987 to Prague and Warsaw. The "Velvet Revolution" of December 1989 had not yet occurred and in Prague when I departed my flight from Munich, I was greeted by a machine gun-wielding soldier. Walking the streets of Prague, I noticed cans of Cuban pineapple for sale in shop windows. Yet, I stayed at a Marriott Hotel that had recently opened.

On the weekend prior to the fall of the Berlin Wall, I was in Warsaw, Poland.

It was clear that a major opportunity to engage in business in East and Central Europe was occurring and I began a journey helping Polish anti-communist leaders to reap the harvest of the fall of communism. They had projects, but no money. I assisted them in financing their projects.

Fortunately, I had good contacts in Poland.

When managing a small office for Boston University College of Communication in Washington, DC, I was introduced to Peter Mroczyk by David Bruce. David's father was a distinguished public servant who had served as U.S. Ambassador to France from 1949 to 1952, U.S. Ambassador to West Germany from 1957 to 1959, and U.S. Ambassador to the United Kingdom from 1961 to 1969. Ambassador Bruce also served as the first United States emissary to the People's Republic of China from 1973 to 1974. David's mother, Evangeline Bruce, was a doyenne of Washington society.

Their son, David, was a gracious conservative who conducted a salon of his own in the Georgetown area of the District of Columbia. On late Friday afternoons, when some were playing golf, he would host movement conservatives, members of congressional staff, visiting foreign officials, and representatives of the policy and think-tank culture of Washington at his townhouse for drinks.

David suggested that I meet Peter Mroczyk, son of a Polish aviator in World War II and an English mother. Peter was among the few native Polish speakers who spoke perfect, accent-less English. He was in Washington working for Radio Free Europe and was a close associate of Solidarity leaders in Lech Walesa's circle. As a result of that introduction, Peter and I worked on several projects assisting his colleagues to reap the rewards of the fall of the Soviet Union.

When Poland's president, Lech Walesa, visited New York for the first time, Peter acted as his translator and I found myself, on November 17, 1989, in the foyer of Forbes Magazine in New York where Walesa appealed to those listening to send money to Poland. Standing behind me was the newly elected Mayor of New York, David Dinkins, whose face expressed concern that someone was in his city seeking money that Dinkins wanted. He was clearly not happy that financing was going to fly off to some faraway place in Eastern Europe. Frankly, I was of a different turn of mind. I felt that the West had abandoned the countries of Eastern and Central Europe to the Soviet Union and that what little we could do to assist their recovery was right and just.

In 1995, four years after the collapse of the Soviet Union in 1991, however, even cautious—and let's face it, politically ignorant—investment bankers on Wall Street were convinced, finally, that a new era had begun. I realized that I didn't speak their language, did not have a business or management degree from Wharton, Kellogg, or Chicago, and couldn't compete with them on the level of the "basics" you learn in those programs. I was self-taught and had to find something to do that represented what I knew best.

Nevertheless, I am amazed what one person can achieve, if he believes in what he is doing and wants to finance his efforts.

Here is a list of a few of the projects I helped finance.

Antenna One Television Group, Warsaw:
Made presentations on behalf of Antenna One to major media companies in the U.S. and successfully recruited a New York investment firm. They recruited Time Warner, Capital Cities/ABC and Turner Broadcasting System as venture partners. Financing totaled $45 million.

US WEST International. London/Bonn:
In 1990 and 1991, Mroczyk and I represented this U.S. regional Bell operating company [RBOC] in its efforts to compete for two Polish mobile cellular telephone licenses.

K & K Medicplast. Warsaw:
This private company, founded in 1985, manufactured disposable, sterile, infusion kits and other plastic medical products. In 1990,

K & K retained me to find an American manufacturer of medical supplies to establish a joint venture to manufacture new medical products for the domestic Polish market.

CAP Farms Ostrow Wielkopolski, Poland:
In December, 1994, I recruited and led a team of three U.S. poultry industry leaders to investigate the possible acquisition of a Polish state poultry processing company in Poland. Equity Financing from the AFL-CIO's Poland Fund: $5.4 million.

Krol Indyk, Swiebodzin, Poland:
Organized a joint venture with Langmo Farms of Litchfield, Minnesota, under the name of "King Turkey" to develop a fully integrated turkey growing, processing and marketing company at an existing state company in Swiebodzin, Poland. Services performed on behalf of Krol Indyk included survey and negotiations with Polish processing companies, representation to key Polish government ministries, preparation of a complete business plan and financing.

There were three main difficulties that I had to contend with in doing business in Poland. The first was poor health. Living under difficult conditions in communist Poland led to poor health and cardiac arrest. After a while, I analyzed the potential for success of a project on the basis of not only what was proposed, but how healthy the entrepreneur was who proposed the project.

A second problem I had to deal with was alcoholism.

On my first flight into Warsaw, a person across the aisle from me pulled out a bottle of vodka and took a drink before our flight landed. A major project we had undertaken was destroyed when a government executive who approved of what we were doing became drunk and crashed his government car. He resigned the next day and all our work came to nothing.

And a third problem was a deeply ingrained corruption. Former communist apparatchiks wanted to become what Poles called "instant millionaires" and attempts to obtain government contracts required paying bribes. I refused to violate the U.S. Foreign Corruption Practices Act (FCPA) and had to decline several opportunities to contribute to the "instant millionaire" fund. On one occasion after making a proposal to a manager of a company that I wanted to privatize, the manager told me that he wouldn't let his company be sold "from Warsaw." On the train ride back to Warsaw, the train stopped unexpectedly. A man of enormous size came to my compartment and a conductor pointed toward me. The thug sat next to me thus reinforcing the manager's threat. This deal, or I, was dead.

As a result of my sojourn in turbulent post-Communist Poland, I came to a firm appreciation of privatization of public sector services. I looked for a way to utilize my hard-won knowledge of how to privatize the many American government services that dominate America's economy. It is common for partisans of both political parties to complain about the failure of the government to invest in infrastructure. Of course, there are not enough tax dollars to pay for the upkeep or construction of all the bridges, tunnels and roads needed to accommodate population growth in the United States. Public roads, airports, bridges, water and sewer systems, the U.S. Postal Service, and the FAA's outdated air traffic control system, as far as I am concerned, should be selectively sold, transferred to, or managed by private sector interests. And younger Americans should be given the option to manage a portion of their payroll deposits to the U.S. Social Security Administration in private wealth management accounts.

I had hoped that what I saw in Poland, when a massive transfer of state ownership to private ownership occurred, could be encouraged in the United States. In Poland, state companies with little to no chance of survival were lumped into "bad company" funds and sold to the highest bidders who then sold off buildings and manufacturing plants, and started new companies from pieces of old ones.

I decided to attempt to establish an Institute for Privatization. At first, I tried to find a university that shared my enthusiasm and I gave presentations to the University of Miami and Florida A&M. But I had not done any fundraising and these institutions, like all colleges and universities, are not buyers, they are takers.

New Internet technologies were low-cost, however. My constant companions, as early as 1987, were an Apple computer, America Online and MCI Mail which I used to communicate with contacts in East and Central Europe. I found that I could send a Telex via e-mail and arrange for my Polish contacts to have an English translator present when I called or visited them.

In 1999, with the support of Massachusetts entrepreneur Ray Shamie, I created a website called "American Academy of Privatization."

After eight years of searching for financing of projects in Poland, I realized that I could not compete with major investment banks who, finally, understood that East and Central Europe were permanently free from Soviet domination, and began to do deals that were well beyond my ability.

What should I do?

Since I knew a great deal about the privatization of government services and state companies, I posted lectures on water and sewer privatization, privatization of the FAA's air traffic control system, and airport privatization.

When I looked at the completed website, I realized that this had the potential to become an online college or university. It was 1999, web browsers were now well-established, and I decided to create what became the first Internet University that featured courses in government, economics, business, and the Liberal Arts taught by conservative academics.

The election of Ronald Reagan created a groundswell of interest in conservative ideas and policies. Hundreds of new tax-exempt organizations were formed, all seeking donations from a handful of conservative foundations. Some of these foundations were controlled by neoconservatives with their own agenda, and I was not familiar with any who were interested in creating a startup Internet university.

By chance I encountered Dr. Henry Manne, founder of the Law and Economics program at the University of Miami. Dr. Manne's center was devoted to the development of the field of Law and Economics. I told him about my plan to found a new, conservative university and he directed my attention to the for-profit University of Phoenix.

I hadn't given thought to the corporate form of my new university, but the idea of starting as a for-profit institution had appeal. With that scrap of information and distaste of seeking charitable, tax-exempt, donations from foundations, I set about founding Yorktown University as a for-profit education company incorporated in Virginia and approved by the State Council of Higher Education for Virginia (SCHEV).

My academic interests were broader than my expertise in privatization of public sector companies, and I conceived of Yorktown as a place where serious scholars could continue teaching when they reached retirement age and younger scholars could remain active in their chosen professional fields even if they were unable to obtain a university appointment.

In my own case, I had attained academic tenure at a Catholic college that had lost its religious bearings in the 1960s and gave up its required curriculum in response to declining enrollments. This was not the institution at which I intended to spend my teaching career, so when opportunity knocked and I was given an opportunity to work in the Reagan administration, I left my tenured teaching position and never returned.

I was, and am, of the view that little can be done from within educational institutions to recover what was lost during the 1960s and 1970s—too many faculty factions have a stake in the current conditions, and too few university administrators have the courage to take unpopular stands and risk losing their jobs. But, if education entrepreneurs can enter the education marketplace and actually compete directly for students with established institutions, that competition will reshape how higher education is conducted in the United States.

Most of us do not set out to achieve great reforms in issues of great importance. We are more often minor players in larger events beyond our control and only later do we see our actions in the larger context. That was my experience on my way to rescue higher education from the Left University.

6. Origins of Yorktown University

In the colonial era, colleges were formed for the purpose of education in classical languages and in ideas and learning necessary to understand the word of God and the uniqueness of America and Protestant Christianity. Most were founded by Protestant religious groups, Congregationalist, Presbyterian, Anglican.[22] Georgetown University, founded in 1789, was a portent of the important role that Catholics would play in American higher education. In the nineteenth century, these early colleges were followed by Methodists, Baptists, Lutherans and other Protestant religions. During that era some Catholic religious formed colleges for Catholic immigrants.

James Piereson in "The Left University" observes, "The purpose of these institutions was to shape character and to transmit knowledge and right principles to the young in order to prepare them for vocations in teaching, the ministry, and, often, the law."[23]

Russell Nieli writes, "Even state-sponsored colleges and universities in the eighteenth and nineteenth centuries had a distinctly Christian religious flavor to them. With the elites of the day harboring a very different view of desirable church/state relationships than those that reign today, the public colleges in America usually reflected the attitudes, values, and world-view of Protestant Christianity, although one stripped to its essentials and devoid of many of the divisive theological doctrines that had led in the past to denominational strife."

This religious orientation began to be loosened as German Idealism was carried to the United States by Transcendentalists. German idealism is a form of humanism rooted in the idea that man is, essentially, God and that history is moving towards consciousness of this divinity of man. The Idealist humanism of American Transcendentalists coupled with Darwin's *On the Origin of Species*, published in 1859, plus the devastating impact of deaths and injuries inflicted upon combatants during the American Civil War that challenged Christian beliefs shaped a secular American nation. That, in turn, changed the character of American universities into the twentieth century.

By 1960, whatever was formerly understood to be the purpose of education had been largely forgotten, and higher education in the United States began a slide down a very slippery slope. Student demonstrators challenged restrictions on free speech, required courses, and the insensitive way that large state university systems treated their students. There were common grievances at the University of California at Berkeley, to cite one example. Students complained that it was possible to earn a degree at most state universities and never have personal contact with administrators or even faculty. Students were treated like ciphers—mere Social Security numbers—and were happy to depart with a diploma, if not an education.

The "Free Speech" protests against limits placed on fundraising for civil rights groups at UC-Berkeley elided into protests against the draft and the Vietnam War. A vehicle was found that would challenge the New Deal coalition created by FDR, the social order of the United States and, particularly, the education establishment and compulsory military service.

Though I opposed the Communist takeover of Vietnam, I myself did not volunteer for service in Vietnam. I had worked for Barry Goldwater and despised Bill Moyers, Secretary of Defense Robert Strange McNamara and, especially, President Lyndon Johnson who lied to the American people about prospects for winning the Vietnam war. Fortunately, I qualified for student and, later, teacher deferments, but tens of thousands of young men of my generation were vulnerable to be called up to fight Lyndon Johnson's war in Vietnam.

LBJ was a New Deal Democrat and a representative of the World War II generation that responded to the call for military service to defeat America's enemies in Europe and Japan. LBJ assumed that the generation of young people living in the United States twenty years after World War II would act similarly.

He was dead wrong.

Many years later, I was walking down Wisconsin Avenue in Georgetown in DC and spotted Secretary McNamara walking toward me. All my thoughts about his conduct of the war in Vietnam came to mind. As I approached, it was clear he knew I had recognized him, but I said nothing. McNamara's, and LBJ's, decisions about the conduct of the war in Vietnam had disastrous long-term consequences for our system of higher education.

As campuses were torn by rioting students, college administrators cowered in fear and caved in to student demands. Revolutionary changes occurred: power was shared with students who could evaluate their professors, sit on boards of trustees, participate in hiring decisions, and otherwise express uninformed views on virtually any subject related to their education. Student evaluations of faculty led to serious grade inflation and traditional required curricula were dropped and cafeteria-style education introduced.

Higher education in America began slowly to break loose from its moorings, and trends leftward that began in demonstrations against the Vietnam War were strengthened with newer claims by feminists, proponents of multiculturalism, and calls for affirmative discrimination and "diversity"[24] that in later years we would call "political correctness."

The move to the Left in American higher education has been demonstrated in Dr. James Piereson's previously cited essay, "The Left University."

Piereson reviews how traditional education became politicized. The central ideas of most colleges and universities constitute what Piereson calls "a bizarre universe in which big-time athletics, business education, and rigorous science programs operate under the umbrella of institutions that define themselves in terms of left-wing ideology." In other words, the purpose of education has been replaced by indoctrination, some subtle and some not-so-subtle. As such, this left-wing ideology is anti-American and anti-business. Though calls for "diversity" are everywhere, intellectually the Left university is closed to non-leftist views.

Jonathan Haidt, professor in the Stern School of Business at New York University and founder of "HeterodoxAcademy.org" writes that "things began changing in the 1990s as the Greatest Generation (which had a fair number of Republicans) retired and were replaced by the Baby Boom generation (which did not). ... [I]n the 15 years between 1995 and 2010 the academy went from leaning left to being almost entirely on the left."

Starting a new Internet university, therefore, was my way to contribute to the recovery of academic standards that were jettisoned in the late 1960s and early 1970s, to affirm the search for truth by opposing a relativism now dominant in American culture, and by creating a community of like-minded conservative scholars.

They were not hard to find.

I had a long association with the Intercollegiate Studies Institute from the end of my freshman year in college when I attended an ISI summer school at C. W. Post College. The weeklong event was led by Russell Kirk and featured visiting lectures by Lemuel Boulware, General Electric's vice president of labor and community relations from 1956 until 1961, E. Victor Milione, president of ISI, and M. Stanton Evans, associate editor of National Review and a contributing editor to Human Events.

When, later, I needed conservative scholars to teach Internet-delivered courses at Yorktown University, I contacted the Faculty Associates of ISI. Seventy responded and fifty were selected to develop our first courses.

My discussions with prospective faculty, then and now, revealed that maintaining high standards in academic courses was not easy. Grade inflation was rampant, and most lived in isolation from scholars who shared their concerns and values—even though many were teaching in large public research universities. I admire their fortitude, their commitment to scholarship, and their ability to function when everything around them seems diminished by intellectual and cultural decline in standards.

But my timing for bringing us all together to found a new university was terrible!

The "dot-com bubble" was about to burst just a few months after Yorktownuniversity.com filed a public offer of common stock. Our SB-1 registration was made effective by the U.S. Securities and Exchange Commission and twenty-five states in November 2000. By February 2001, the bottom fell out of the high-tech dot-com market and I withdrew the public offer.

In 2000 I had contracts with fifty faculty members willing to develop courses in exchange for a contract to teach those courses and common stock. We had to obtain Virginia approval to use the name "University" in our stock registration, and we went to market without a curriculum installed in a course delivery platform and without students.

That wasn't necessarily a bad thing, since one may dream about doing something that requires millions of dollars—but without financing the venture remains a mere dream.

My attempt to obtain between $1.25 and $2.5 million in a registered direct public offer of common stock in a company with little to show prospective investors wasn't entirely wrongheaded. A direct public offer is the sale of registered securities directly to the public without the mediation of a securities broker. In the right economic climate with the right public relations and a pre-screened list of prospective investors, direct public offers can be registered and successfully carried out on less than $150,000. Legal and accounting fees and state registration costs can total $100,000 and the balance goes to company agents who telephone prospective investors. By contrast, the cost of a public offer marketed by a securities broker can easily cost $2 to $5 million and much more.

Still, our initial effort was not successful. We sent copies of our Prospectus to 4,000 conservative donors, held several press conferences at the National Press Club, but the public wasn't buying. In retrospect, that was probably due to the bursting of the dot.com bubble and a general sense that we would not be able to attain accreditation.

Perceived barriers to accreditation surely were part of the failure of our stock offer, but I believe that by the year 2000 the

American conservative intellectual community had been demoralized and weakened in mind and spirit. Opposition to Progressives seemed pointless. A general sense that "they" had won demoralized us all.

Many conservatives who believed in limited government, a strict construction of the Constitution, and the beneficial working of free markets, did not connect education in those principles with their social effectiveness. Some believed in "spontaneous" order and lacked appreciation for cultural currents that do not right themselves spontaneously.

Conservatives had lost, if they had ever known, an understanding that their precious heritage had to be preserved through education.

Though cable television, talk radio, and Internet blogs are a means of dissemination of conservative ideas, our ideas must first be created and nourished. It is extremely difficult to engage in original research outside the confines of academic institutions, and through interaction at colleges and universities between students and those who profess ideas, knowledge and science. Ignore that and you lose your culture and, ultimately your country and your freedom. That is the situation in which citizens of the United States today find themselves.

Here is a representative sample of colleges that may be called "conservative" in the sense that they offer required courses across a range of disciplines and are committed to "education" as opposed to "training."

Traditional Liberal Arts
  Hillsdale College (MI)
Christian Liberal Arts Colleges
  Pepperdine University (CA)
  Grove City College(PA)
  Ave Maria University (FL)
  University of Dallas (TX)
  Biola University (CA)
  Franciscan University of Steubenville (WV)

Regent University (VA)
Liberty University (VA)
Wyoming Catholic (WY)
St. Bonaventure(NY) Concordia (MI)
Mt. Saint Mary's (MD)

Great Books

College of the Arts and Sciences (Internet)
St. John's College, Annapolis (MD)
St. John's College, Santa Fe (NM)
Thomas Aquinas College(CA)
Thomas More College of Liberal Arts (NH)
Gutenberg College (OR)
George Wythe College (UT)
University St.Thomas (MN)

This is a nation of more than 330 million persons and more than 3,000 colleges and universities. If a mere 1% of all our colleges and universities are conservative and the remainder to varying degrees are representative of the "Left University," we are in very deep trouble.

Mainline higher education had long abandoned true education and commenced transformation of university "education" into a vehicle for vocational training programs. Here is a list of training programs in which students can earn expensive, four-year, academic degrees at a typical public university

Bookkeeping
Athletics & Athletic Training
Business Administration
Communication
Computers
Counseling
Dance
Decision Sciences
Drawing & Design
Exercise Science & Wellness

Fashion Merchandising
Film
Geographical Information Systems
Graphic Design
Industrial Technology
Information Science
Information Systems & Technology Instructional
Design & Technology
Lifespan & Digital Communication
Marketing
Media & Multimedia
Occupational & Technical Studies
Painting
Performing Arts
Physical Education
Programming
Project Management
Recreation & Tourism Management
Sport Management
Theatre & Dance
Visual Arts

It doesn't take much imagination to see that many of these skills can be taught at lower cost via the Internet by corporations or vocational schools and through apprenticeships. Except for students seeking employment in public education and government, there is no need to enroll in costly degree programs for vocational training. And many parts of these programs can be taught while students are in high school.

No nation can long survive that neglects education as Americans have in the twenty-first century. That understanding motivated me to found a conservative Internet university.

7. Distance vs. Classroom Instruction

Those of us associated with the founding of Yorktown University had a great idea, a willing faculty, the technology to deliver courses in low-cost delivery systems and other off-the-shelf software, and we had seed money from a handful of investors who believed in the venture.

But we didn't anticipate that the dot-com boom would be over by the time we had organized marketing of our registered public offer. Nor did I, or even Bill Gates, appreciate that new technologies that brought about changes in other industries would not have the same impact in higher education as they did in less regulated industries. Gates writes, "While video and computers have become important educational tools, their overall impact has been quite modest. There's good reason to be humble about technology in education."[25]

I could and did quickly master the system of higher education regulation, but it took much longer to realize how great is the distance between classroom instruction and distance learning. The solution was better instructional design.

But I had my mind on other things, including the first steps toward founding an online university, mastering state authorization regulations, recruiting staff and faculty, and working with faculty to design course content for Internet delivery. What I didn't do was ask whether our new Internet courses "worked."

I had ignored that the modalities of classroom instruction and distance learning via computers are strikingly different.

I had gone to traditional universities and taught in traditional college classrooms, but I didn't know that Internet education is quite different from what transpires in classrooms.

A typical college course at a campus-based institution requires that students attend class for fifty minutes of instruction three times a week for fourteen weeks. Thirty-five hours are eaten up by sitting in classrooms. A mid-term and final exam are given and a required term paper is due at the end of fourteen or sixteen weeks. Student coursework is then graded and grades are submitted to a Registrar where they accumulate credits based on hours upon hours of classes. At the end of this process, usually consisting of forty courses, a student receives a degree. Transcripts of coursework are sent to prospective employers and young college graduates launch their professional careers.

Internet courses are different. There is no personal interaction, or very little, between student and instructor, and students more likely are working adults in their late twenties and sometimes in their forties. They are employed and want to improve their work situation by qualifying for management positions. Though accreditation and Title IV regulations require discussions that demonstrate interaction between students and instructors, in reality, online discussions simply don't work. It is simply not possible to discuss much of anything online with groups of students, and even discussions with one or two students take so much effort that few instructors stay at it.

How then can an Internet distance-learning university such as Yorktown University contribute to higher education reform?

At the start, we asked our instructors to design courses into ten sessions and to record lectures for each of those sessions. We gave each a Sony mini-disc recorder, a supply of discs, and when they had recorded their lectures, they returned the discs and a staff person edited them for access in each course.

I was preoccupied with financing this enterprise and trying to market Yorktown University even though it was not accredited. But, we enrolled our first ten or more students in May 2001 and blithely assumed that things would work out.

Well, they didn't.

Our Introduction to Constitutional Law course was designed

at a level that most students who hadn't learned the basics of American government couldn't understand.

Live discussions with students—common in Constitutional Law courses, were soon found to be impossible to organize online. Later, we learned that students didn't listen to recorded lectures, and courses that were designed to be completed in ten weeks took fifty weeks—or more—for our students to complete.

In other words, we had the wrong "instructional design" for Internet delivery of courses. About this time, the U.S. Department of Education under Margaret Spellings instituted a requirement that each course demonstrate the "Learning Outcomes" of each session. We were now being directed "from on high," that our traditional syllabus had to identify and demonstrate the "outcomes" of "learning" of each session of our courses. Moreover, those outcomes had to be stated in "value-neutral" terms.

Appendix D contains a list of the value neutral-terms we were required to use to describe what our students learned in every course. These words are not designed to articulate growth in character, wisdom and knowledge, or patriotism and civic responsibility. They are words that describe "things," not qualities of soul, intellection or understanding.

Nevertheless, if we wanted to attain accreditation, we had to comply, and we set about revising every syllabus for every course.

We took this opportunity to retain the services of several instructional design professionals, adjusted their concept of instruction to our concept of education in the Liberal Arts, and designed a six-session course to guide classroom instructors in developing effective online courses. We reduced the number of sessions of our courses to no more than eight, and made other adjustments to make them effective.

Since we offered courses in the Liberal Arts, including philosophy, religion, ethics, political philosophy, history, art history and architecture, we had to carefully present course content without overwhelming our students.

In doing this, we created a successful model for distance learning in the Liberal Arts that few institutions with Internet courses have achieved.

That failure is evident in the very low numbers of students who earned academic credits for completion of MOOCs when introduced at Arizona State. ASU's President created a partnership with Harvard/MIT's edX program. "Less than 1 percent of the learners in the massive open online course partnership between Arizona State University and edX are eligible to earn credit for their work, according to enrollment numbers from the inaugural courses."[26] Harvard's edX MOOCs, as well as the first three companies[27] to enter the high-tech MOOC marketplace, were designed by classroom instructors in computer science or, in the case of Harvard, engineering.

They created very efficient learning management systems that are capable of enrolling infinite numbers of students (one enrolled 160,000 students the first time it was offered) but so poorly were these MOOCs designed that few students chose to complete a course of study.

When the first MOOCs were introduced in 2011, every one of them ignored the reality that distance learning cannot replicate classroom instruction. As a result, completion rates in MOOCs hit rock bottom.

Here is my explanation of why the first MOOCs developed by Udacity, edX, Udemy and Coursera were educational disasters:

MOOCs Are Not TV. Anyone who visits a Coursera, Udemy, Udacity or other MOOC course will see immediately that somebody thinks that video recordings of lectures are useful. They have some utility, especially for the scholars who, until the advent of MOOCs, lived in obscurity. Now they are hailed at airports and on the walkways of their campuses as celebrities. Students compelled to watch these recordings, however, wonder when they'll end. Time is an ingredient in the success of web-based distance learning because it takes less time to complete a course online than it does in a typical semester of classes. So, if less time is the attraction, why add more time to MOOC productions by requiring students to watch home movies?

Don't Ask a Traditional Instructor to Design His Own MOOC. In fact, don't ask a classroom instructor to engage in anything but instruction. So, asking one of these specialists to design a course for one of the most difficult modes of learning—distance learning—is a recipe for disaster. That, of course, is one of the reasons that in the footrace for survival in the twenty-first century, the MOOCs will win.

Oversight Is King. Most distance learning simply operates on cruise control. A content specialist develops a course, students enroll and the specialist thinks his work is done. As a result, student surveys give distance learning mixed grades, but seldom a solid "A" for excellence. And the reason is that traditional colleges do not oversee instructor/student engagement on a daily basis. For every instructor of an Internet-delivered course there has to be a person who monitors course activity.

Training Students and Instructors. Most course management systems are simple enough to learn, if you can type and know the fundamentals of word processing and e-mail communication. Leaving aside the development of multiple-choice quizzes and entering grades in an electronic grade book, most systems are easy to use. Unfortunately, the habit of checking e-mail, attaching files to messages, and saving files cannot be assumed. Even some web browsers don't work on all course management systems, and then there are differences between Macs and PCs. When you add to that microphones for use in Webinars, suddenly you are consuming valuable time that ought to be used in instruction. Every company offering MOOCs must have a system for training students and instructors.

The Web Is a Resource. Even today, some instructors will advise students to subscribe to the print edition of the Wall Street Journal or require books that must be ordered for delivery by mail. Few will surf the web for valuable resources or create exercises and drills that utilize website content. Surfing the web is a habit that older instructors have not acquired. Encouraging them to "think" online is as important as it is for filmmakers or television producers to think "pictures." The language of training is words. But distance learning is a mix of words and web-based images. Overcoming "word think" is imperative for a successful MOOC.

Discussion Topics Are Not Essay Tests. Because most training professionals come from a classroom environment, every Internet course they develop contains "threaded" discussions. Sometimes these discussions can work, but only if the topics to be discussed are not tests or essay assignments disguised as topics. And even then, a good topic requires a comment, a response. and another comment on the response. In practice it is very hard to keep an online discussion going without a) monitoring interaction, and b) designing topics that generate discussions and require expensive instructor engagement.

Should MOOCs Offer Discussions? A natural response to a new medium of communication is to adopt the practices of traditional communication. In higher education, that means having discussions. One of the reasons the first MOOCs have low retention rates is our tendency to do what we learned to do in traditional classrooms even though some of those practices clearly do not work online. MOOCs are open to anyone with access to the Internet and offered without instructor engagement. For that reason, if we follow the best practices of effective online learning to their logical conclusions, we will seek alternatives to discussion fora.

Students Can't Write. Instructors will tell you that most of their students are not adept at writing. Unfortunately, Internet distance learning requires that students be able to write or, at least, communicate by means of grammatical sentences. The aspiration of the creators of the first MOOCs to provide education for everyone will quickly face the difficult truth that not everyone can write a grammatical sentence. MOOCs designed to prospect for employees will weed out those not qualified for employment—before they are employed.

Students Will Cheat. In any environment where there is no supervision, some students will plagiarize or cheat on quizzes.

Solutions such as iris scans, fingerprint IDs, or video surveillance come to mind as ways to assure that every student submission is verified. That, however, adds to the cost of MOOCs. The solution is to accept that it takes a commitment to fraud that is difficult to sustain over time. Sustaining fraud over a series of MOOCs will experience less cheating than single MOOCs. The lesson to be drawn is not to require costly anti-cheating devices that drive up the cost of MOOCs, but understand that some students who enroll will cheat. Minimizing single-event cheating may be achieved by not offering "Badges" for successful completion of only one course.

Age Is An Issue. Any company or college seeking to utilize the efficiencies of MOOCs must be aware that Internet browsers revolutionized how Americans conduct business, purchase products and communicate. But, the first web browsers were not commercially viable until the late 1980s. A late fiftyish-age instructor who was born thirty years before the advent of web browsers probably began to use a PC only in the last ten years. He is not trained properly to lead development of, or even participate in, an online training program. Best to look for someone between the ages of 25 and 35.

Most Instructors Are Not Geeks. Any course management system that requires course developers to learn computer programming is dead as a doornail. Only course management systems with user interfaces that enable everyone to install content into a course template will survive. Some of the best MOOCs have mastered this aspect of the business and deserve praise for transcending their "geekness."

8. The Role of the States in Higher Education

If the difference between classroom education and distance learning were not enough of an obstacle to the educational success of Yorktown University, the higher education regulatory environment was the king of obstacles.

Unfortunately, American higher education is highly regulated not only at the state and local level where bureaucracies and bureaucratic mentalities dominate but, now. also, at the federal level.

The States

The word "education" is not found in the Constitution of the United States for a reason. Education was a prerogative of the states. But, gradually, education came under the oversight, and now the control, of the federal government.

We used to say that "Federal money means federal control." Nowhere in American society is this more true than in higher education. But the states have been aggressive in shaping education regulations.

The Southern states responded to federal desegregation that followed *Brown vs. Board of Education* in 1954[28] with massive resistance. Public schools were closed to avoid desegregation and state authorities were created to administer this policy. For that reason, the Southern states, to this day, have very well-developed state authorization boards. Though these authorities are no longer used to disenfranchise African Americans, education authorities in the Southern states have stringent regulations regarding offering courses and degree programs for academic credit. Here are a few examples taken from a directory of state regulations of distance learning that has been published by the State Higher Education Executive Officers Association (the chief executives of statewide governing, policy, and coordinating boards of post-secondary education).[29]

Alabama. "As a prerequisite to program approval, an unaccredited institution requesting to offer degree programs in Alabama must undergo an external review of its programs of study by an outside consultant(s) chosen by the Commission. The unaccredited institution will underwrite all costs related to the external review."

Arkansas. "An institution requesting AHECB certification must provide documentation that the institution is 1) accredited by an accrediting agency recognized by the United States Department of Education or Council on Higher Education Accreditation; 2) authorized to operate as a postsecondary institution in its home state; and 3) has documentation of home state approval and program accreditation for professional licensure programs. An institution applying for institutional or program certification for the first time must not advertise or operate in Arkansas until AHECB certification is granted."

Texas. Any schools offering private postsecondary education must be licensed, with rare exceptions. In addition, degree programs must be approved by the Texas Higher Education Coordinating Board.

Tennessee. Requires authorization of long distance learning. Commission staff evaluation of physical presence required.

Florida. "A licensed institution which is not accredited by a United States Department of Education recognized institutional accrediting agency shall use an enrollment agreement or application for admission which, in addition to the catalog, shall be the binding contract between the institution and the student. The binding document shall include, but not be limited to, the following: (a) Title. The binding document shall be identified by title as a "Contract", "Agreement", "Application" or similar title and clearly indicate that it will constitute a binding agreement upon acceptance by the institution and the student; (b) Name of the institution. Name, phone number, and physical address of the institution; (c) Title of Program. Program title as licensed and identified in the catalog; (d) Time Required. Number of clock hours or credit units, including the number of weeks or months, or credit hours required for completion; (e) Credential for Satisfactory Completion; (f) Costs. All costs shall be clearly stated; 1. Tuition. The total tuition for the program must be listed by the total length of the program, the tuition cost per credit hour, clock hour, term or academic year. 2. Fees. All refundable and nonrefundable fees payable by the student. 3. Books and supplies. The cost for books and supplies may be estimated if necessary. This item may be omitted if the binding document states that the costs for books and supplies are included in the tuition charges as stated in the document. 4. Any other costs. Any other costs required to be paid by the student, whether or not purchased from the school. These costs may be stated as a listing of goods or services not included in the tuition. (g) Terms of payment. The method of payment of all costs shall be clearly stated in the binding document and shall comply with federal and state laws. (h) Class Start. (i) Anticipated Program Completion Date (for Institutions that are not Colleges or Universities). (j) Class Schedule. The day, evening or other schedule of class attendance must be clearly stated (if known at the time of signature by student). (k) Termination or Cancellation by the Institution or Student. Grounds or procedures for cancellation of a binding document by an institution or student shall be clearly stated. (l) Refund Policy. Institutions shall comply with refund policy as provided in subsection 6E-1.0032(6), F.A.C. (m) Employment Guarantee Disclaimer. Institutions shall publish the disclaimer as provided in paragraph 6E-1.0032(6)(j)."

Georgia. The instructional programs "for the online, distance, or correspondence education institution require direct student-faculty interaction through an NPEC approved, formal plan by e-mail, internet, fax, telephone, videoconferencing or other real time means."

Virginia. At Appendix A I've placed a document that criticizes regulations in Virginia that compelled us to move to Colorado. The State Council for Higher Education of Virginia

(SCHEV) is the epitome of out-of-control state regulation of higher education. Under the auspices of a Republican-dominated state board, SCHEV continued the prohibition against use of the word "University" in a company's name without state authorization; required accreditation or movement towards becoming accredited; requires annual re-certification; institution of an annual fee with a higher fee assessed for un-accredited institutions; requires 15 contact hours per credit, thus ignoring the distance between classroom and Internet-delivered coursework; requires annual audits or financial reviews; and imposes a surety bond that covers 100% of tuition payments.

In addition to hostile education regulations, the culture of Virginia is not entrepreneurial. Virginia cities have development programs managed by career executives and supported by appointive members. None is organized to review proposals by trained investment professionals.

As a result, "development" usually means facilitating the purchase or construction of buildings.[30] Since we began Yorktown University in Virginia near the village of Yorktown in York County, I visited York County's Economic Development Office to announce the exciting news that a new university—Yorktown University—was about to come to his small county. The assistant director of the office revealed his bureaucratic bias by asking, "Is that legal?"

The Commonwealth of Virginia has a rigid regulatory system embodied in the State Council of Higher Education for Virginia (SCHEV). Originally created by segregationist Virginia politicians who sought to thwart federal desegregation of public education through massive resistance, SCHEV controls all higher education in the Commonwealth and protects state universities from competition by new entrants into the state's higher education marketplace. Many Virginians living in the Commonwealth today remember when their public schools were abruptly closed. Though public service covers a range of government services, in Virginia SCHEV represents a "legacy of suppression." Jim Crow laws are long gone, but SCHEV remains as an echo: Virginia's most powerful non - elected regulatory agency.

A center of government during the Colonial era, capital of the Confederate States of America, and now geographically adjacent to, and economically dependent on, the federal government in Washington, DC, Virginia is comfortable with, and is a generator of, costly regulations governing every aspect of commerce—including higher education.

If you compare population by state and public employees per capita, the State of New York—not known for principled limited government—has a population of 19.7 million and 88.56 public employees per capita.

The Commonwealth of Virginia, with a population 42% fewer than New York has 77.18 public employees per capita or a mere 8.8% fewer than New York.[31]

Even though in 2000 when we decided to found Yorktown University, SCHEV was dominated by appointees of Republican governors—George Allen and Jim Gilmore— and had shed its desegregationist ways, SCHEV was controlled, as is so much of Virginia state government, by a powerful professional bureaucracy.

Among SCHEV's political appointees was a partner in a Richmond law firm that represented Virginia state public universities. In other words, a member of the higher education regulatory body in Virginia was a partner in a law firm representing public universities regulated by SCHEV.

That is a clear conflict of interest that continues to this day.

The appetite of any permanent bureaucracy to regulate is especially great when an agency has life or death control of those it regulates, and in 2003 SCHEV's bureaucrats had the support of a Republican, appointed by Gov. Jim Gilmore, who was an advocate for more regulations.

Dr. Cheri Yecke, appointed by Gov. Gilmore to serve on SCHEV, believed that federal regulations as they were applied by the federal government to regulate Title IV-eligible universities should be the "standard" for regulation of colleges and universities in Virginia— even those not yet accredited and thus not Title IV-eligible.

While serving on SCHEV, Dr. Yecke also served as the Director of Teacher Quality and Public School Choice at the U.S.

Department of Education for the Bush administration (2002–2003), during which time she was detailed to the White House as a senior advisor for USA Freedom Corps. In 2003, I maintained that this constituted a conflict of interest, since the charter of the U.S. Department of Education forbids the department from interfering in state education programs.

Dr. Yecke was my first look at the big government face of the "new" GOP represented by the administration of George W. Bush.[32]

Though I voted for George W. Bush—in 2000 and 2004—I did not understand that he was subtly undermining the party of limited government.

Excessive spending, a new prescription medicine Entitlement program, and the invasion of Iraq led ultimately to the destruction of the Republican brand and created the political conditions that permitted the election of Barack Obama and the nomination of Donald Trump.

Finally, even I figured out that something was very wrong and, in 2004, I published in Modern Age a major critique of the "New World Order" of American foreign policy advocated by the internationalist faction within the Republican Party.[33]

While the Bush White House was engaged in the destruction of the American national interest by pursuing foreign policies that sought to make the Middle East "democratic," the U.S. Department of Education under Secretary Margaret Spellings destroyed the one agency for accreditation of liberal arts institutions and introduced value-neutral standards for measuring learning "outcomes."

Dr. Yecke stuck her aggressive hand into Virginia and used the levers of power established by Senator Harry Byrd to "protect" Virginia colleges and universities from desegregation and used those powers to protect Virginia education consumers from startup, unaccredited, institutions entering the market with high technology products.

While Dr. Yecke had a good reputation among conservatives because of her advocacy of school choice, she is an "educationist" who is infatuated with government regulations. Educationists spend a great deal of time focusing on the process by which to regulate education, and no time on what education is. She was a perfect fit for the professional educationists who populated SCHEV.

Dr. Yecke worked with the professional staff of SCHEV to increase regulations on unaccredited institutions authorized by SCHEV. New rules that went into effect in September 2003 made it impossible for Yorktown University to continue. I protested vigorously, eventually forcing Dr. Yecke to abstain from voting on new regulations which were ultimately approved, making Virginia "safe" from competition from new companies using high technology to deliver programs for credit at low cost.

Since we could not and did not want to comply with new SCHEV regulations, our Trustees approved voluntarily giving up our Virginia state authorization. In December 2003, we moved to Colorado where we obtained authorization from the Colorado Commission on Higher Education (CCHE).

9. Colorado Here We Come!

We sought and attained authorization by SCHEV to operate in Virginia in 2000 and by May 2001 we enrolled our first students and began growing enrollments in government and economics degree programs. But SCHEV made demands that tuition be placed in escrow until a student completed courses, imposed an annual fee and other financial requirements, and allowed for surprise visits by SCHEV functionaries who had authority to close an institution overnight. This was a state commission dominated by Republican appointees!

The answer was to move—to Colorado! We did experience a sense of loss, however.

A startup education company with limited funds doesn't need the challenge of a move to another state. More important, the inspiration for Yorktown University flows from the blood of patriots shed in the Battle of Yorktown in 1781. Our "brand" reflected the character and virtue of those who sacrificed their "sacred honor" so that we might live in a self-governed, independent, and free nation. And, it expressed our belief in the necessity for civic education. At a time when virtually all proprietary Internet institutions are focused on training for vocations, the focus of Yorktown was training for citizenship.

Nevertheless, we decided to move to the state of Colorado which still, in 2003, embodied the spirit of those who founded the West and maintained a tradition of welcome for newcomers.

At first, we moved in name only. A cousin residing near Durango, Colorado agreed to act as registered agent for Yorktown University. Durango, on the "Western Slope" of Colorado, is a six-and-a-half-hour drive to the Colorado Commission of Higher Education offices in Denver. In winter the roads are dangerous, so we were far removed from authorities who might want to know what this Internet university looked like.

Fortunately, a community of conservative Republicans then dominated the state of Colorado and we were assisted by radio talk show host Mike Rosen, who introduced me to leading Republicans, and Bob Schaffer, a former member of the U.S. House of Representatives who had served on the House Education and Workforce Committee. CCHE was balanced by appointments made by Gov. Bill Owens. Greg Stevinson had been appointed by Gov. Owens the year we obtained CCHE authorization in 2004 and kept a lid on any aggressive actions against institutions moving toward accreditation.

Between 2004 and 2012, we were left alone and enjoyed the freedom to grow investments, attain national accreditation and accredit eleven degree and certificate programs.

Unlike Virginia, where GOP Governor Jim Gilmore did nothing to de-regulate SCHEV, I cannot emphasize how important it was that a coalition of conservatives and Republicans in Colorado supported a "light" state regulatory regime in state education policy. Despite the fact that Colorado's public universities are part of the American Left University syndrome, and though conservative scholars are despised if they seek appointments at Colorado state universities, when we arrived in Colorado there was no attempt to limit what or how we taught our courses.

The curious thing about technologies that can be used to create an online university is this: they are inexpensive.

All you need to enter the higher education market is incorporation in a state ($350), a registered domain ($39), a leased server ($1,800 a year), a PC ($450), a telephone land line ($120 a year), web access ($1,150), one desk and two chairs ($300) and office space ($5,400 a year). State "authorization fees" vary but excluding those fees, a startup Internet university costs under $10,000.

Add your salary, and the cost of someone to answer phone calls, and you can begin your journey into the higher education marketplace.

The year before we began operations in 2000, cable television entrepreneur Glenn Jones attained regional accreditation of Jones International University. That inspired me to accomplish what Jones achieved. But, between 2000 and 2008 only one regional agency accredited solely Internet-based universities.

If I had Glenn Jones's wealth and the knowledge of Internet education that I have today, we might have been one of the six solely Internet institutions to attain regional accreditation before the regional agency with oversight for Colorado closed that door. Nor did I know that Colorado would soon take a Leftward political trajectory after Gov. Owens left office.

But, from 2004 to 2008, we used all our skills and became a very professional online university that attained national accreditation. One shareholder I had not seen for five years sent another investment saying that he didn't think it was possible, but we did it.

I began our transition to Colorado by talking to Governor Owens after a speech in Washington, DC at the Cato Institute in June 2003 and by making contact with Sean Duffy, a member of Gov. Owens' staff. Owens was thinking about a Presidential bid, and Sean Duffy, former executive director of the Commonwealth Foundation in Harrisburg, Pennsylvania and well-connected to the network of conservative policy organizations throughout the United States, was recruited by Owens to strategically place him in contact with conservative leaders. Duffy introduced me to the executive director of CCHE who quickly approved our authorization to offer degree programs from Colorado, as long as we were making progress toward accreditation.

With state authorization in hand I could and did successfully raise operating funds and made several trips to Denver for meetings and to look for a low-cost office. On my first trip, I attended the annual dinner of the Independent Institute, a conservative state policy organization. Past presidents of the Institute included John Andrews, then Majority Leader of the Colorado State Senate, and Tom Tancredo, then a member of the U.S. House of Representatives.

Both were representative of the hard-core conservative base of the Colorado Republican Party, and were persons I reached out to as I made my way through Colorado's political thickets.

Andrews is a "movement conservative" and had published regularly at National Review before winning election to the Colorado State Senate. Tancredo became a leader against illegal immigration long before Donald Trump seized on that issue.

Bob Schaffer had run for Lt. Governor of Colorado in 1994 when the ill-fated Bruce Benson[34] was the GOP gubernatorial nominee. Schaffer, however, successfully ran for Congress from Ft. Collins and served three terms before losing a race for the U.S. Senate in 2004.

From 2004 until Yorktown University was compelled to close in 2016, Schaffer loyally supported it as an elected Trustee.

Still, we needed inexpensive office space. On one weekend, I visited Union Station in downtown Denver's "LoDo" district where office space was for rent. While reading the classifieds in Denver's free paper, I found an advertisement for office space in a building that specialized in small incubator offices. I signed a lease for a one-room office priced at $425 a month and shipped our equipment and furniture to Denver.

We were in business again—just barely—since I still had to figure out how to finance operations. By word of mouth and following leads I was able to identify and attract a core group of original investors. But this was long and difficult work.

Finally, the idea occurred that I should call Raymond LaJeunesse for advice. Ray LaJeunesse, for many years, has headed the Right to Work Foundation. Ray and I had a spent summer at Grove City College attending courses in Economics taught by Hans Sennholz. Ray suggested that I speak to the person who had created the Right to Work Committee's direct mail-fundraising system.

I was attracted to the idea of using direct mail to solicit investments, but U.S. Securities and Exchange Regulations governing general solicitation of investments are quite strict.

First, non-registered securities may be offered only to

accredited investors and direct mail is considered a form of advertising. The Jobs Act of 2012 subsequently loosened the rules by creating a Form D 506c registration for general solicitation of accredited investors, but since 1935, raising funds for non-registered securities was limited to friends and family, and even they should be accredited.

An accredited investor is a person whose assets, excluding his personal residence, total one million dollars.

What was I to do? I had run out of names of wealthy persons to ask for investments. And those who might easily have committed what we needed to found a conservative university were not aware that the Left University was indoctrinating generations of students to hate America and, particularly, American capitalism.

Few businessmen were fortunate to study at universities like Cornell, where Clinton Rossiter and other conservative scholars including Walter Berns, Allan Bloom, and Werner Dannhauser taught the ideas of the Founding Fathers and their philosophy of limited government. Nor had many studied with Leo Strauss at the University of Chicago where Chicago's Jewish community supported conservative scholars like Frank Knight, Ronald Coase, George Sigler, Milton Friedman, Arthur Laffer, Allen Bloom, Frederick Hayek, and Saul Bellow.

Most businessmen, if they earned a college degree, studied Business Administration or Economics, more likely than not taught by Keynesian economists. One of Yorktown University's shareholders told me that it took him twenty years to recover from the economics he learned at the University of Michigan.

Others who did donate to conservative causes were attracted to the growing number of conservative think tanks or to the few established conservative colleges like Hillsdale or Grove City.

In other words, scholars of conservative ideas had little financial support from our business classes. Several times I heard a businessman dismiss my request for investments with the phrase, "Those who can, do; those who can't, teach."

Moreover, there were very few conservative foundations and even fewer were dedicated to scholarship. In my view, many of these "conservative" foundations wanted to "use" academics to achieve power or position and sponsored "policy" studies, but not humanistic scholarship. The Earhart Foundation was a lone exception and can take credit for contributing to the survival of scholarship by conservative scholars.[35]

Though J. Howard Pew was known to support Grove City College because it featured free-market economics, I was told that Henry Regnery had to beg Pew for $5,000 to help pay for the publication of Russell Kirk's *Conservative Mind*. Later, the Pew Foundation that J. Howard established would turn its back on his principles and use his wealth to support every idea he had disdained in his lifetime. The Ford Foundation is another example. That led the founders of the John M. Olin Foundation to shut down rather than to trust the next generation of executives.

Perhaps for this reason, one of the most important developments on the Right occurred outside American higher education—the Supply-side economics movement gave new life to the GOP through the influence of Howard Jarvis, Art Laffer and Ronald Reagan in California; Jack Kemp and Richard Rahn in New York; Cong. William Steiger of Wisconsin; and the Supply-side economists on the staff of the Joint Economic Committee including Steve Entin, Paul Craig Roberts, Bruce Bartlett, and Allan Reynolds at the "Kemp Commission."

The history of GOP politics from Taft to Gerald Ford was characterized by a focus on deficit reduction. Republicans would complain about excessive spending, win elections, raise taxes to reduce deficits, and lose elections.

Supply-side economics largely ignored deficits and focused on cutting income and capital gains taxes. Supply-siders argued that what was important was proportion of spending to gross domestic product. Even if spending increased, if the economy grew and the deficit relative to GDP was lowered, we had made a significant achievement.

One of the leaders of Supply-side economics was the founder of Club for Growth, Steve Moore. Soon after Moore established the Club, in 1999, he held a fundraiser at his home which I attended. Much to my surprise, many of my colleagues in the conservative movement were also there. Steve Moore had tapped into a deep vein in the conservative movement in the United States, and in 2004 I held a full-day presentation of supply-side economics at FreedomFest in Las Vegas. Present were Steve Moore, Mark Skousen, Stephen Entin, Alan Reynolds, and George Gilder.

In 2005, I decided to approach former Congressman Pat Toomey, who succeeded Steve Moore as head of Club for Growth. I explained to Toomey that Yorktown University featured Supply-side economics and I explained what we had to do to achieve accreditation. He seemed to realize for the first time how difficult is the accreditation process, but he agreed to stand for election as a Yorktown Trustee and he gave me his endorsement of our Supply-side economics program.

I featured that endorsement by Pat in direct-mail fundraising appeals until he asked me to stop when he ran for the United States Senate in 2009. I never mailed to more than 300 persons at a time, and only to those whom I could identify as qualifying as "accredited." Nevertheless, direct mail and Pat Toomey's endorsement saved Yorktown University.

As an example, one day I was alone in our Denver one-room office and the telephone rang. I answered and the person on the line said, "Do you have a physical address? I don't send checks to Post Office Boxes." I assured the caller that, indeed, we had a physical address and in fact I was there at that moment taking his call.

The next day, I arrived at the office shortly before 9:00 am and upon opening the office door, I saw on the floor a Federal Express envelope. Inside was a check for $100,000.

Only direct mail found this investor and it saved the entire enterprise and sustained our efforts to attain accreditation and market our degree programs.

10. The Role of Accreditation

Accreditation is like a government passport. With a passport, you may travel to a foreign country. With accredited status, institutions may offer college courses for degree credit.

And because all states require that institutions be accredited—or are moving toward accreditation—in order to qualify for state authorization, the accreditation agencies recognized by the U.S. Department of Education are the gatekeepers who decide who may enter the higher education marketplace.

In December 2005 the American Academy for Liberal Education (AALE) informed Yorktown University that it would accept an application for pre-accreditation of our undergraduate liberal arts degree programs. We set about to transform our standards to meet those of the AALE, and in December 2006 we prepared for a site visit. Early that month, U.S. Secretary of Education Margaret Spellings chose not to renew recognition of AALE as an accrediting association.

Spellings, who became Chancellor of North Carolina's public university system in 2016, was President George W. Bush's instrument for higher education reform.[36] Unfortunately, AALE stood in the way of those reforms.

The American Academy for Liberal Education was founded to accredit high quality liberal arts institutions, particularly Great Books institutions, whose purpose is to educate in the Liberal Arts by studying the great ideas of the Western tradition. AALE had no interest in developing assessments that would quantify and measure learned behaviors. Even the value-free word "behavior" was repugnant to AALE's leaders, who understood that human beings "act," and animals "behave." That led to a brawl between everyone not given to educationist methodologies and the U.S. Department of Education.

At the time, I did everything I could to save AALE. I drafted appeals for shareholders to send faxes to the Department of Education. I organized a briefing for congressional staff and made personal visits to offices of members of Congress. Other conservative academics were active, too. Dr. Larry Arnn, president of Hillsdale College visited the White House but found no support.

To this day, I wonder what motivated Education Secretary Spellings to do something so contrary to the conservative base of George W. Bush's political support. Some say that Sara Martinez Tucker, Under Secretary of Education in the Bush administration, disliked AALE's president, Dr. Jeffrey Wallin. Others thought that AALE's reporting was deficient, and some suggest that the decision by AALE not to accredit Patrick Henry College led the politically connected Evangelical Christian founder of that college, Mike Farris, to ask President Bush to withdraw AALE's recognition. A born-again Christian, "W" would have been sympathetic to Mike Farris's complaint.

Whatever the true reason, Yorktown University was dealt a devastating blow. Not only had we organized for pre-accreditation by AALE, but we wanted to be able to show prospective students that they could take our online courses and later transfer to some of the best liberal arts colleges in America.

In the summer of 2007, with AALE's position hopeless, we moved on and prepared our courses and all the paperwork for submission of an application for accreditation by the Distance Education and Training Council, from whom we finally attained institutional accreditation in June 2008.

If we were to continue to operate in Colorado, we had to be accredited or moving toward accreditation. So, though DETC was a terrible "fit" for Yorktown, we had no choice.

At Yorktown University, at a cost of about $3,000 per course, we re-tooled every degree program and course in our curriculum to fit into a mold that defines the learning outcomes of every course. Multiply that $3,000 times every course offered for academic credit at every degree-granting institution in the U.S. and you gain a sense of the enormous cost of the Bush administration's social engineering. That was in 2008. In January 2016, I spent a day at Colorado University-Boulder and learned that eight years later, CU had still not complied with U.S. Department of Education learning-outcome regulations.

Compliance is costly. but if you are big enough, you can delay complying. Philosophically, however, the task of compliance with "Learning Outcome" regulations is repugnant.

In order to state what a learning outcome is, we were compelled to use the language of behaviorism by using value-neutral verbs to describe each learned behavior. Students don't learn, understand, or appreciate; they define, compare, contrast, and analyze.

These emasculated learning outcomes devalue what education is all about and revive what Eric Voegelin described as the "derailment" of philosophy by propositional metaphysics.

In my own courses in the history of political theory, I have described the learning outcomes of every session. Listed are the conclusions described in behavioral terms of some of the greatest intellectual events that have occurred in the West—the break from mythic consciousness, the turning around of the soul depicted in Plato's Myth of the Cave, the discovery of the mind, the comprehension of the human person in relation to transcendent divine reality, the measure of what is right and just, and the formulation of the Western concept of a limited state.

In stating these conclusions as learning outcomes I have "reified"—made into things—experiences of reality that have no "thingness," that cannot be defined in terms of learned behaviors, but nevertheless are the source of all that we admire in Western civilization. I have been directed by the U.S. Department of Education to engage in a process of hypostatization by which truth, justice, God, Heaven, and Hell become things about which we can debate.[37]

In other words, the germ of the derailment of philosophy in propositional metaphysics, the reification and hypostatization that closes the soul to experience of reality, is official policy of the U.S. government.

This periodically occurs in great civilizations—the trial and death of Socrates, the school of Legalism in China, Scholasticism in late medieval Europe, behaviorism in post-World War II America, and the recent rise of political correctness are all examples of intellectual currents that close inquiry, transform educational content into process, and reify that which are not things—but this is the first time in memory an apparatus of the administrative state responsible for education in America has mandated the closure of the mind.

Regional accreditation, what some inaccurately refer to as "full accreditation," was organized in 1885 when the established colleges and universities of the day organized the nation into geographic regions. If an education entrepreneur desires to create a university that is regionally accredited, he must make application for accreditation with the regional agency responsible for accrediting academic institutions in the state in which he is domiciled.

For one hundred and thirty-two years, only one regional accreditation agency has ever accredited an institution that did not operate from a physical campus. Despite the ridiculousness of this requirement, no political party has recommended breaking up the regional agencies. American political parties are part of the "system."

Why, for example, in an age of mass communication should the United States be organized in geographic regions for the purpose of accreditation? And why must an institution be accredited by a Title IV-authorized accrediting agency to offer Title IV loans to students, if they have no intention of offering access to federal tuition loans and grants?

New technologies employed to enter the education marketplace run smack into a government regulatory and accreditation process that is cumbersome, outdated, costly, and intentionally designed to protect members of a cartel of accredited colleges and universities.

From 1999 to 2008, only a few solely Internet-based startups made it to regional accreditation: Jones International University, Northcentral University, Western Governor's University and

American Public University to name four. They are all domiciled in the region of the Higher Learning Commission (HLC), sometimes referred to as "North Central."

The headquarters of the Higher Learning Commission is in Chicago and extends from West Virginia in the East to Colorado in the West. HLC is the regulatory "big enchilada" of American higher education accreditation. Beginning in 1999, HLC granted regional accreditation to Jones International University.

The founder of Jones University, Glenn Jones, was the billionaire owner of Jones Cable that offered educational courses on cable TV late at night. On a trip to Washington, DC where Jones was a member of the Advisory Board of the Library of Congress, he visited the Vietnam War memorial. Sitting on a bench with a view of visitors to the memorial, Jones was inspired to create a low-cost Internet institution that would benefit military veterans. He invested $164 million dollars of his own money in Jones International and was the first solely Internet university to attain regional accreditation.

In March 2015, Jones International University was closed as a consequence of gainful employment regulations imposed by the Administration of Barack Obama. Glenn Jones, age 85, died five months later and Yorktown University lost a friend with whom we worked to protest regulations that CCHE imposed in 2012. The "good times" for for-profit education in Colorado and the United States had come to an end.

The location of the Higher Learning Commission of the North Central region was significant. Senator Barack Obama had taught at the Midwest Academy, a socialist institution for training aspiring community organizers in the revolutionary tactics of Lenin.

Lenin's 1902 essay "What is to be Done?" outlined the methods that would achieve revolution. They included a) maintaining large non-Party organizations with mass membership controlled by communists, b) concentration on agitation of single ideas to foment discontent and c) organized activism aimed at "the masses," not exclusively the "proletariat." Black Lives Matter is such a "non-Party" organization.

President Obama hated for-profit education and it became obvious to the leadership of the Higher Learning Commission that any further accreditation of for-profit Internet institutions could not occur during the new Obama administration.

In 2009, anticipating that changes at the Higher Learning Commission might occur, I asked two members of our professional staff to attend a pre-accreditation seminar conducted by HLC in Chicago. Upon their return they mentioned that HLC-accredited institutions would be required to be authorized in all the states. I thought they were misinterpreting what they heard, ignored their report, and continued to plan to make application for regional accreditation by HLC as soon as we improved enrollments and income.

In April, 2010 I attended that same seminar conducted by the Higher Learning Commission. This was the second such seminar I attended in order to prepare Yorktown to apply for regional accreditation.

Until 2008, the Higher Learning Commission was a trendsetter, the only regional accrediting agency willing to accredit institutions that teach mostly or entirely over the Internet. A few months before the election of President Obama, however, Dr. Sylvia Manning became president of HLC, and policy changed. No longer would HLC accredit solely Internet-based institutions.

At the April 2010 seminar I attended, Karen L. Solinski, vice president for legal and government affairs, informed the seminar that not only must all accredited institutions be incorporated in one of the states in the region but they must have a state license in each state in which they have a "substantial presence."

During the break I asked Ms. Solinski to specify what constitutes "presence" in a state. In good lawyer-like fashion she asked me, "Do you have representatives in any states?" I said "no." Her raised eyebrows suggested that I did, and I thought, well, we do have instructors who reside in and instruct our students from states other than Colorado, where Yorktown University is incorporated.

She then asked, "Do you have proctors in states?" I replied, "Yes, but surely you aren't saying that the use of a proctor triggers a state licensing requirement?"

She said that it would.

Proctors supervise the exams taken by students in online courses. Solinski seemed to be saying that merely having a student taking an exam, and thus having a proctor monitor it, whatever the state, would require our university to have a license in that state. In addition to the cost of multiple state licenses, each state has its own regulations. Some states require annual fees, others require a hefty surety bond, and Virginia even taxes authorized shares of stock companies. Keeping track of them would be costly, time-consuming, and difficult.

During a break, I asked Solinski, "Do you mean that HLC intends to enforce state licensing regulations?" She said, "Yes." This means that HLC, a private organization, is taking on the responsibility of enforcing regulations promulgated by the states. Not only is this inappropriate but it is probably unconstitutional.

I called to Solinski's attention a Federal Trade Commission finding that it is a restraint of trade for states to require out-of-state optometrists to be licensed if they sell contact lenses in the state. The example seemed to be exactly parallel. To my comment, Ms. Solinski replied, "Education is a special responsibility of the states."

Okay, education has historically been the responsibility of the states (the U.S. Constitution doesn't mention education), but regulating private companies from other states is not a recognized state responsibility, whether the companies are in education or not.

During this seminar, I was sitting at a table along with two representatives of another institution also accredited by DETC. They were shocked by this exchange. I explained to them that the Inspector General of the Department of Education had informed the Higher Learning Commission in December that its recognition could be revoked. According to the Department, HLC had endangered its status "because it granted accreditation to a for-profit university despite a single flaw that the inspector general deemed to be serious."[38]

The issue of state authorization of Internet-delivered courses is critical to the expansion of distance learning courses and programs for degree credit. A virtue of the Internet is that it is boundless and does not recognize state lines. A natural, borderless, market has been created that achieves economies of scale that can lead to lower prices of goods sold via the Internet. The regional accreditation agencies, supported by policies initiated by the U.S. Department of Education, support enforcing regulations designed to protect consumers by balkanizing the borderless Internet market into geographical regions.

It is incredible, but the Obama administration encouraged state authorization regulations that require Internet education companies to be authorized in every state where they have a presence.

After first being introduced in 2010, a U.S. federal court ruled against them. The U.S. Department of Education then attempted to reintroduce state authorization regulations in 2014, but that attempt floundered on a requirement that the states conduct an "active review" of out-of-state colleges. In July 2016, the U.S. Department of Education attempted to reintroduce a state authorization regulation that does not require "active reviews" by the states, and promulgate it before the Obama administration leaves office. The Department failed.

What has been missed in all public discussions of these proposals is the underlying attempt to bring the education authority of the states under the authority of the federal government. If states carry out compliance reviews of federal regulations, then the education authorities of the states come under the control of the federal government. The federalization of higher education financing which has been in development since 1965 becomes federalization of all higher education in the states.[39] That, I believe, is the surreptitious purpose of all proposals for regulating for-profit education introduced by Deputy Under Secretary of Education Robert Shireman and is the reason, I believe, that this one political appointee was the most dangerous appointed executive in American government since U.S. Attorney General A. Mitchell Palmer conducted raids against immigrants suspected of disloyalty.[40]

11. The Federal Government and Higher Education

If barriers to accreditation—national or regional—were not sufficient, in 2009 Robert Shireman, the new Deputy Under Secretary of Education for Policy in the Obama administration, commenced the introduction of new, punitive, regulations designed to destroy, or at the very least cripple, for-profit education in the United States. Soon after being appointed in 2009, Robert Shireman gave a speech to the National Association of State Administrators and Supervisors of Private Schools (NASASPS).

Here is a list of the publicly-traded companies cited by Shireman on April 28, 2010, the percentage increase in income from Pell Grant funds that Shireman thought was excessive, and the share price of these companies the morning of July 6, 2016 compared to the day Shireman gave his speech:

Colleges Shireman Cites in Speech	Pell Grants	Share Value April 28, 2010	Share Value July 6, 2016
Corinthian Colleges[41]	38%		
DeVry	42%	$ 59.55	$18.66
ITT	44%	$105.62	$ 1.83
Strayer	95%	$221.53	$48.50
APEI	44%	$ 44.43	$26.81
Kaplan[42]	33%		
CECO	29%	$ 33.41	$ 6.13
EDMC	16%	$ 22.69	$0.025
Capella	40%	$ 90.82	$52.20
Grand Canyon[43]	55%	$ 24.85	$39.02
Bridgepoint	61%	$ 25.65	$ 6.15
University of Phoenix	9%	$ 61.50	$ 9.05

Robert Shireman is thought by Ohio State University economist Richard Vedder to be "the only guy I ever met whose very appointment to public office destroyed hundreds of millions of dollars in wealth."[44] Unfortunately, Shireman's policies have been vigorously pursued by the U.S. Department of Education even after he resigned in July 2010 and even though the Department's Inspector General commenced an investigation of Shireman of ethics violations involving allegations of conflicts of interest.[45]

Robert Shireman became active in higher education reform as Legislative Director to Senator Paul Simon (D-IL). During his seven years on Simon's staff, Shireman got his first taste of blood by successfully negotiating assistance for victims of fly-by-night trade schools. "Fly-by-night trade schools" is Shireman's own description from his LinkedIn account, and suggests that he was predisposed to assume that for-profit education was characterized by deception.

He next spent two years as a Senior Policy Advisor on President Clinton's National Economic Council where his focus was on education of low-income families and Hispanic families, middle-class tax cuts for education, and increases in funds for Pell Grants.

Shireman then served four years as Program Director at the James Irving Foundation where he was responsible for $15 million in annual grants.

Shireman next founded the Institute for College Access & Success where he focused on enrollment and graduation policies affecting disadvantaged students in higher education. Though Shireman's lifelong interest was "education," apart from earning the Ed.M. degree from Harvard in Teaching and Curriculum, there is no indication that he earned an advanced degree in a substantive academic discipline other than "education," nor that he ever taught a course in any subject at the college level.

When Shireman was appointed Deputy Under Secretary of Education he brought to his tasks a specialization in education "process." Unfortunately, that orientation was motivated by animus toward for-profit education.

In April 2010, Shireman gave a speech (Appendix B) to a meeting of the National Association of State Administrators and Supervisors of Private Schools (NASASPA). These are the executives responsible for education in the fifty states. In that speech, Shireman sarcastically called attention to the growth in Title IV Pell grants by for-profit companies.

NASASPA brings together all the "state boards, commissions, agencies or departments that are engaged in the administration, regulation, or supervision of private schools, colleges, or universities."

If you want to affect the states in their administration of their education authority, this is the group to meet. Shireman's message: the federal government and the states cannot rely on accreditation to assure that taxpayers and the public are protected. The states should step up their role in regulating higher education. For any state regulator, those words are music to their ears. But what are the long-term consequences?

Shireman initiated regulations that may be called "Obama's Nine Commandments.

1) break up a free market in education products delivered to education consumers by the internet;
2) promulgate regulations that close or severely limit access to Title IV loans by students attending for-profit Internet institutions;
3) limit the amount of student loans that may be borrowed to pay for tuition in programs based on future income derived from employment gained by completion of those programs. For example, if a program costs $100,000 and annual income for employment in that fields is $28,000, students may not borrow more than actually can be repaid
4) define academic credits in terms of serial time (inputs) as opposed to what students learn in a course taken for credit (outputs), thus requiring Internet providers to demonstrate that students and instructors are engaged in serial time equal to their counterparts in classroom-based institutions;

5) require that every state institute regulations that compel institutions not domiciled in a state to comply with state licensing requirement of every state in which they have students or instructors;

6) threaten regional accrediting associations that if they permit transfer of ownership of failing non-profit colleges to for-profit companies, their federal recognition as an accrediting agency will be revoked;

7) threaten regional accrediting associations that if they accredit another for-profit Internet institution, their recognition as accrediting agencies will be revoked;

8) initiate criminal inquiries aimed at for-profit institutions by the U.S. Justice Department, the U.S. Securities and Exchange Commission, the Consumer Financial Protection Bureau, the Federal Trade Commission and encourage the Attorneys General of the states to conduct criminal investigations of for-profit institutions; and,

9) initiate well-coordinated attacks on for-profit education companies by members of Congress who allege massive abuses by for-profit institutions.

Slightly fewer than the Ten Commandments that Yahweh gave to Moses, the Obama administration's "Nine Commandments for 'Reform' of Higher Education" were instituted without legislation by the Congress of the United States in a process called "negotiated rulemaking."

First developed by the Department of Labor in the Ford administration, negotiated rulemaking is a way to promulgate regulations by convening parties to meet with government agency representatives and negotiate new rules. The Negotiated Rulemaking Act of 1990 that authorized this process was given an injection of steroids by Robert Shireman who used it to completely reorganize the way the U.S. Department of Education regulates for-profit education.

Regulations were implemented without a whisper of dissent by public and non-profit colleges and universities. Perhaps that was the case because powerful members of Congress supported them. One of these members of Congress was Senator Dick Durbin (D-IL). In 2010, Senator Durbin gave a speech to the National Press Club in which he outlined a broad plan to attack for-profits in the following steps:

> **Denying** access to federal grants and loans to schools that have defaults of 30 percent over three years or 40 percent in one year
>
> **Restricting** "institutions that receive federal student aid from paying their admissions recruiters on the basis of enrollment numbers"
>
> **Instituting** "new regulations that would require for-profit colleges to disclose job placement rates"
>
> **Relating** student loans to "gainful employment." If degree programs do not lead to good jobs that enable student to repay student loans, then the institutions offering those degree programs will lose access to federal tuition assistance programs (this regulation has been proposed)
>
> **Restricting** the use of federal financial aid dollars that can be used for "slick advertising," such as "billboards, television commercials, and advertisements on the sides of buses"
>
> **Controlling** how much these institutions lend to their own students
>
> **Stopping** the practice of buying accredited institutions.
>
> **Lowering** the 90-percent threshold that allows schools to receive up to 90 percent of their income through federal programs

Though aimed at for-profit education companies, all but the last two of these measures could be applied to non-for-profit private institutions, if they protested too much.

The application of new regulations by negotiated rulemaking brought the University of Phoenix, ITT, Career Education Corp,

DeVry and other for-profit, regionally accredited education companies to their knees.

Recently, the National Advisory Committee on Institutional Quality and Integrity (NACIQI), a principal education advisory body established by Congress to advise the Department of Education, recommended that recognition of the American Council of Independent Colleges and Schools (ACICS) be withdrawn.[46] Previously the focus of the Obama administration's executive action was to destroy for-profit education companies. Action against ACICS took the attack to a new level by destroying a national accrediting agency that accredited mostly for-profit schools from the education marketplace. That affected 245 colleges and 800,000 students enrolled in ACICS colleges. Few of those colleges will qualify for regional accreditation.

12. "Smart Money" and Higher Education

I did not comprehend when I founded Yorktown University that the smart money, well- heeled investors with an interest in education, didn't engage in the startup of new universities—they bought regionally accredited institutions that were on the ropes.

Institutional investors and billionaires interested in the education marketplace live in another world. All have bought their way into the marketplace at enormous cost by purchasing nationally and regionally accredited institutions.

Michael Milken invested in Cardean University that purchased the nationally accredited ISIM and attempted to develop an Internet MBA program on that platform. Though accredited by the Distance Education and Training Council (DETC), credits earned are not transferrable to regionally accredited universities, and Milken moved on to greater opportunities.

The investors behind Grand Canyon University purchased a failing Baptist college and have taken that asset public in a successful registered security offer. Before doing that they offered to purchase a community college in Arizona with 60,000 students for $400 million.

Randy Best founded Whitney International University and purchased Chicago's Barat College. That, too, didn't work out. Douglas Becker, founder of Sylvan Learning, has grown Laureate University by purchasing foreign institutions, but not before he ran into the regulatory buzz-saw that governs for-profit universities in the United States.

Most of these, and some other investors, are in the education business because they have access to hundreds of millions of dollars—not because they know what education is all about and want to work to reform higher education.

This is their story.

I'll start with one observation and move through a short list of millionaire investors in higher education starting with Randy Best.

The ability to buy accredited colleges did not assure success, but the experience led them to develop and market services that traditional colleges lacked. As the regulatory environment in the United States tightened—particularly after 2009— their wealth was focused increasingly on education opportunities in foreign countries.

Of all those cited below only Douglas Becker, who founded Sylvan Learning, understood what is involved in "education" and understood higher education regulations. The others entered this market because it appeared at the time to be a good investment. Those hopes were dashed in 2009 when the Obama administration commenced its attacks on for-profit higher education.

Randy Best

I start with Randy Best because his name was mentioned, by chance, in a conversation with a prospective investor from Texas. I had researched this investor's political donations and verified that he was a political conservative. When I called and explained to him what we were attempting, he told me that he would have to ask Randy Best before he would invest. He had done well in an education investment recommended by Randy.

Best started an investment bank with an early supporter[47] and became interested in higher education through "Higher Ed Holdings." That was a vehicle for Best to provide online courses for Lamar University and expand to other institutions in Texas under the name "Academic Partnerships." The website of Academic Partnerships lists six services that the company offers to partner institutions:

Market Research & Strategy
Academic Services

Partner Support
Marketing
Enrollment Services
Retention Services
Strategic Partnerships

Most traditional colleges and universities offer four services: classroom instruction, hotel and food services, and entertainment (football). Organized as guilds, they know little about online course-delivery design, very little about marketing, and assume that the stream of new enrollments they enjoy will always assure sufficient resources to sustain these institutions. In a rapidly changing higher education market, Academic Services offers professional management services that these traditional institutions lack.

Who is Randy Best?

The website of Best Associates states, "Randy Best is Chairman of Best Associates and has founded or acquired more than one hundred private or publicly owned businesses."[48] Among the businesses he has founded are Voyager Expanded Learning, Whitney University Systems, and Academic Partnerships. Whitney University Systems offers centralized services from offices in Argentina and Colombia and is evidence of the international focus of some of the wealthiest education entrepreneurs.

Though the many courses and online degree programs developed by Academic Partnerships are impressive, there are few signs of any attempts at "excellence." The company's website praises the company for advancing "the mission of democratizing education" by making education accessible and achievable.

The idea of making education accessible is a theme that appears often when new technologies are applied to education and expresses the positive goods that can be attained by education companies organized for profit.

The entry of MOOCs into the higher education marketplace was also trumpeted by language usually associated with revolutions. The "human right" to a college education championed by these new MOOC ventures implied that traditional higher education, as currently organized, is denying individuals a fundamental human right.

The concepts of a human right and democratization of education are highly charged, even emotional. But upon closer scrutiny, democratization implies that, somehow, education is something that can be "democratized."

Does that mean that everyone, irrespective of ability, deserves a college education?

Unfortunately, since American higher education is now totally dependent on subsidized student loans, democratizing education means giving everyone the opportunity to support a bloated, contradictory, bureaucratic higher education system by incurring large amounts of student loan debt.

Michael Clifford

Perhaps one of the most flamboyant of education entrepreneurs, Michael Clifford is outspoken and daring. Growing up, he played trumpet and other horns in bands, smoked pot, did crack and drank a lot. But, then Clifford experienced a religious conversion and became a practicing Christian. He had a gift for fundraising and worked for Christian organizations. Bill Bright, founder of Campus Crusade for Christ, encouraged him to think about the education business. A friend in Phoenix introduced him to the founder of the University of Phoenix, John Sperling, and Clifford was hooked.

Michael Clifford is best known for purchasing a distressed, regionally accredited non- profit Baptist college, converting it into a for-profit university, and successfully conducting in 2008 a registered securities offer of stock in Grand Canyon University. Later, I received a telephone call from Clifford expressing interest in Yorktown University. He liked our courses and said they may fit into his plans at a university where the faculty begged him to purchase their college before it went under. That venture did not work out and in 2013 Clifford launched "Dream Degree," a program of courses, some of which have American Council of Education (ACE) recommendations "for academic credit." That

means that colleges willing to accept ACE credit recommendations for successful completion of Dream Degree courses will attract students to enroll in their institutions. When enrollments are
slipping, recruiting Dream Degree students is an option to consider.

Michael Milken

Milken is associated with the term "Junk Bonds." During the
Carter administration, interest rates rose to 20%, making it difficult for entrepreneurs to finance business startups or acquisitions.
Enter Michael Milken, who made risky high-yield bonds popular
and thus "created" capital that would otherwise not have been
available for growing companies or starting new ones.

Milken's first entry into higher education was limited to an
investment in Cardean University that acquired DETC-accred-
ited ISIM, an online business degree program. Milken's true interests, however, seem to be K-12 education. Milken founded
Knowledge Learning Corporation (KLC), a subsidiary of Knowledge Universe, with Oracle CEO Larry Ellison, which owned a
for-profit child care provider, KinderCare. Milken also founded
K12 Inc. that provides online services to charter schools. Like
Randy Best, Milken and his brother Lowell have focused on education. Lowell Milken writes, "Education is at the heart of
nearly everything we value as individuals, as citizens and as
productive human beings. The centrality of education to realizing human potential, contrasted with the grim reality of inade-
quate educational opportunities for far too many of our nation's
youth."[49]

Larry Ellison

With Michael Milken, Oracle CEO Larry Ellison founded Knowledge Universe with an investment of $500 million in 1998 and
owned or invested in companies that operate schools, including
Knowledge Learning Corp. and Nobel Learning Communities, a
network of private schools. Knowledge Universe owns a majority
interest in LeapFrog Enterprises. In 2014 Knowledge Universe
launched an association of major universities offering massive,
open, online courses (MOOCs) in business subjects.

Douglas Becker

Douglas Becker, founder of Sylvan Learning, entered the higher education marketplace with greater understanding of education as a business than any of his millionaire colleagues. After selling Sylvan, Becker founded Laureate Education that now operates seventy-five schools in thirty countries. Becker was swept up in the problems of Hillary and Bill Clinton for retaining the services of the former President to serve as Chancellor and spokesman for Laureate.

After encountering difficulties in operating Internet-based institutions, these wealthy investors focused on providing services to existing colleges and the purchase of colleges and universities outside the United States. As Yorktown University discovered, acquiring skills necessary for effective distance learning are difficult to learn and in the case of those who "bought" accredited colleges, impossible to master without actually gaining operating experience in distance learning. Nevertheless, we can hope that, after Obama administration regulations attacking for-profit higher education are replaced by more sensible regulations, or revoked, these men will return to the domestic United States internet education market and participate in the reorganization of higher education after its creative destruction and satisfy education consumers who have rebelled against high tuition costs of the education cartel.

13. What It Costs to Enter the Higher Education Marketplace

I didn't have the finances of Michael Milken, Larry Ellison, Randy Best, Michael Clifford or Douglas Becker. By May 2001 Yorktown University had "burned" about $200,000 and might have achieved profitability in two or three years were it not for barriers to accreditation. In June 2008, seven years after we had enrolled our first students, we had burned $1.75 million. At the end of our long journey, we had burned $4 million. Without barriers to accreditation, we would not have burned more than $1 million to establish Yorktown University and grow enrollments into several thousand.

Much of the $4 million in financing was expensed to meet the cost of state and federal government regulations and meeting "standards" of accrediting agencies. That is an example of the costs associated with the unique system by which America accredits academic institutions. What is seldom appreciated is that accreditation has little to say about quality. Accreditation affirms that an institution is qualified to access federal Title IV funds.

There were other unknowns we faced that, taken individually, were surmounted with hard work, persistence, and the support of generous and devoted shareholders. But, had they been encountered in one fell swoop, there wouldn't have been a Yorktown University.

Choosing the right form of incorporation of a for-profit education company is critical. Only a stock corporation gives you the latitude to expand and seek new investments without approval of partners. Limited Liability Companies offer the tax advantage of writing off losses from personal taxes, but higher education is always more costly and new tranches of financing will be required. It is not advisable to have to ask limited partners for permission to raise new money and thus dilute their holdings.

Where you incorporate is also important.

Virginia, like some other states, assesses an annual fee for stock authorized. Since you may want to grow your company by selling additional stock, at the start it is a burden to pay an assessment for four million shares of authorized stock.

Delaware is often preferred as a state of incorporation, but annual franchise fees based on stocks issued can be burdensome. The tax laws of each state must be considered when considering where to be domiciled.

Since for-profit education companies have come under increased scrutiny, it helps if a state has a stable political climate dominated by conservative Republicans.

Any map that identifies which states are dominated by Republican governors and which are Democrat Party-controlled, will indicate where to start in finding a state where your college is best domiciled.

Each state has its own higher education regulatory authority and SHEEO, the State Higher Education Executive Officer Association, publishes an online directory of all regulations affecting distance learning.[50] A review of that database will tell education entrepreneurs what the annual registration fees are and the reporting requirements of each state.

Some state regulations are odd. For example, Florida requires that online courses assign only the latest edition of textbooks! Every year, each company authorized must appear in person at an annual meeting of the state's board and answer any questions asked by staff or appointed Board members.

Of concern is the fact that the regional accrediting agencies do not accredit solely Internet-based institutions, thus blocking competition from potentially low-cost, high-tech providers. The system is structured, however, to permit nationally accredited institutions to offer access to Title IV grants and loans. That assures that tuition will seldom be priced at a level lower than the maximum amount students may borrow.

Yorktown University did not resist this tendency, and though we never obtained Title IV access, we did participate in a Department of Defense program that permitted active duty military to use Tuition Assistance benefits, which at that time were priced at $750 per course. Instead of pricing our tuition at $250 per course, we raised it to the maximum level of TA, and, effectively, cut off any opportunity for enrollment growth by being the low-cost provider.

That was a mistake. Taking eight years to learn how to develop a college level course for effective distance learning and then over-pricing our first accredited degree programs, plus the banking crisis of 2008 that dried up risk capital for more than eight years, led to withdrawal of Yorktown University accreditation by the Distance Education and Training Council in 2012.

14. Fighting the Higher Education Establishment

The threat of competition from Internet education providers challenges the way that traditional universities conduct business: how they price products, control costs, and educate students. Yes, most universities have Internet websites. Most faculty members, though not all, use computers; and some courses are posted online to supplement student course assignments. But traditional bricks-and-mortar institutions have not reorganized how they operate and conduct their business as a result of these new technologies. Because of regulatory barriers there is no incentive for traditional institutions to change their mode of operation. Attempting to compete with them requires extraordinary dedication to education or insanity. Nobody—at least no sane person—engages in the startup of new universities in the United States because of new, efficient, low-cost technologies, despite the benefits they can bring to educating consumers.

To give some insight into the political obstacles that startup institutions using new technologies face when attempting to break into the education marketplace, I'll recount a story about a meeting I had in December 2002.

The late Joann Davis, Congresswoman from York County, Virginia, was responsive to my complaint that since we were located in the region of the Southern Association of Colleges and Schools (SACS), we could not aspire to regional accreditation. Her experienced chief of staff took me to visit the education staff person of Buck McKeon (R-CA), then chairman of the House Education and Workforce Subcommittee on 21st Century Competitiveness. I explained our predicament: that Yorktown University was an Internet institution based in Virginia, but SACS didn't accredit Internet institutions.

He laughed.

I later received an email message from him informing me that he had joined a K Street lobbying firm.

Our guide from Joann Davis's office then took me and a staff member to meet with a member of the professional staff of the House Education and Workforce Committee. I had learned from John Barth, the U.S. Department of Education staff member in charge of the recognition of accreditation associations, that the renewal letters of recognition of five regional associations was in draft form. I argued that a delay would cause these associations to inquire about the holdup, and he could then respond that there is some concern that they are not accrediting Internet institutions. I asked what would happen if he didn't send the renewal letters. Mr. Barth told me he would be fired.

So up to Capitol Hill I went to ask "George," a senior staff member of the House Education and Workforce Committee, whether we could do this. He said, "That would jeopardize the process." Well none of us back then wanted to jeopardize the process. We just wanted to expedite the accreditation of Yorktown University, so we didn't press the matter.

But shortly after Christmas I began to think about how I could jeopardize the process. After the New Year, I called the House Education Committee and asked to speak to George. I was told that he was no longer on staff. George was now employed by the California State University system in its Washington office. Members of congressional staff use their positions as way-stations to lucrative private sector employment as lobbyists. This is a fact of life and deters necessary reform.

Nevertheless, I made presentations to Congressional and Committee staff several times. Because the Title IV loan program is the principal reason college tuition costs have skyrocketed, in a meeting with the Republican staff of the House Education and Workforce Committee I suggested that one way to reduce reliance on Title IV was to send a percentage of all Title IV funds to the states as block grants. Staff members present were not enthusiastic about that idea.

Yet, if conducted with adequate preparation and strict guidelines, the States could benefit by creating their own subsidized loan programs for in-state students without the regulatory requirements that limit access. States might decide to sponsor vocational programs and direct those funds to institutions in their states that offer low-cost programs that lead to employment. Or, states may choose to benefit liberal arts colleges or reward corporations that create their own training programs by offering to subsidize tuition cost of students learning skills needed by participating corporations.

A shift from accredited colleges to corporations offering practical training leading to employment is necessary, if the power of the education cartel is to be challenged. This will not be easy to accomplish without direct subsidies.

Several years ago, John Allison, then recently retired as president of BB&T University, graciously introduced me to the staff of his bank's "University" in Winston-Salem, North Carolina. BB&T University has its own campus and offers training programs for management employees.

I offered to develop—and accredit within four years—an Associate Degree in Banking for BB&T to offer junior and senior high school students in communities they serviced with the promise of employment to the top students successfully completing the program. I argued that it did not require a BA in Business or Economics from Duke, UNC or any other regionally accredited university to perform the functions of an entry-level bank teller.

One of the two men told me that they wanted persons who knew how to dress and a college degree was evidence of that. In reality, my proposal was radical and would have challenged the ability of BB&T University to manage teenage junior and senior high school students, many of whom would be female.

The goodwill that BB&T would have earned in the communities it served was lost because BB&T University managers only wanted to do what they had been doing. A subsidy of $400,000— to create and accredit an in-house BB&T Associate Degree in Banking—might have persuaded them to take the risk.

15. Resurrection—Thirteen Ways to Reform Higher Education

A perfect storm developed near Bermuda on October 27, 1991. Named Hurricane Grace, by October 30 it caused 40-to-80-foot waves. If the equivalent of a perfect storm hits American higher education it will require that waves of education consumers who reject going into debt resist borrowing to pay tuition. Alumni donations and state subsidies will decline and traditional colleges and universities that are overextended will not make timely loan payments on buildings they felt they needed to attract students.

When that occurs, possibly as many as one thousand regionally accredited colleges may not be able to make payroll.

Since education has been in decline for decades in the United States, we need not worry that higher education will suffer. American higher education has already been reduced to mere training.

I expect that when corporations—and organizations on the Right and the Left—like the Service Employees International Union (SEIU) or the United Auto Workers (UAW), or think tanks like the Heritage Foundation, Intercollegiate Studies Institute, and the Cato Institute buy their own institutions or enter the education marketplace with their own college programs, we will be very close to retaking higher education from the Left University and the government-recognized accreditation agencies.

For example, many privately held companies are owned and operated by businessmen who appreciate free market capitalism. If the Heritage Foundation were to offer a "Certificate in Free Market Capitalism" and offer these businesses the opportunity to offer courses in this subject to their employees, a new way to enter the workforce will have been created.

Employers may want to give preference to hiring prospective

employees who successfully demonstrate that they know that entrepreneurs create markets, that low taxes encourage economic growth, and that lowering regulatory barriers creates economic opportunity.

It is my firm conviction that a market mix of technologically advanced for-profit colleges, tax-exempt think tanks offering subject-oriented certificate programs, and corporate training programs are necessary for the resurrection of American higher education from the ashes of a coming creative destruction.

By lowering the importance of academic "accreditation," or completely eliminating it by creative state and federal legislation, a free market in competing education products can be created in which education entrepreneurs can begin to shape the future of American higher education.

Here are thirteen ways this can be accomplished:

1. Prohibit members of Congress and congressional staff from employment with colleges or universities.
2. Repeal the Negotiated Rulemaking Act of 1990.
3. Direct the regional accreditation agencies to accredit institutions from outside their "regions."
4. Direct the regional agencies to immediately recognize solely Internet-based institutions for accreditation.
5. No longer require institutions not participating in Title IV programs to adhere to U.S. Department of Education Title IV regulations.
6. Lower the percentage of three-year default rates from 30% to 20%. Institutions with three-year default rates of 20% will immediately lose access to Title IV programs.
7. No longer permit regional agencies to accredit Internet-based programs and recognize a new national agency for accreditation of Internet delivered programs.
8. Charter an agency solely for the accreditation of MOOCs and adjust Title IV regulations to permit offering MOOCs for degree credit, if an institution offering MOOCs chooses not to participate in Title IV.
9. Shift Title IV funds to the States in block grants.

10. Encourage the States to subsidize corporations that create training programs.
11. Abolish NACIQI or reform its method of appointing members.
12. Abolish the U.S. Department of Education.
13. Form an "Education Consumer Revolt" political action committee.

1. It is offensive when members of Congress or congressional staff members with authority to make or interpret regulations governing higher education leave government service and work as lobbyists for education interests. It is time to prohibit members of Congress and congressional staff from all employment with colleges or universities and their lobbying arms. I understand the appeal of appointing former members of Congress to serve as college or university presidents, but at a time when the system of higher education is broken, it does no one any good when former members of Congress "work" the broken system to their personal advantage.

2. In light of the growth in power of agencies of the federal government, if we are to recover the principle of limited government, we must repeal the Negotiated Rulemaking Act of 1990. There is no need to provide an administrative avenue for going around the Congress of the United States and make regulations by fiat. The notion that there is any significant "negotiating" that occurs in the "negotiated rulemaking" process is a sham. Our federal government agencies are no longer ours; they are the personal hobbies of professional bureaucrats who use them to increase their own power.

3. The time has passed when accreditation should be overseen by agencies organized according to geographical regions. So also is the practice of granting regional accreditation only to institutions offering programs from physical campuses. The Federal Trade Commission should be directed by Congress to bring restraint of trade actions against the regional accreditation agencies.

4. If that action is ineffective, the U.S. Secretary of Education should be directed to require the regional agencies to immediately recognize solely Internet-based institutions for accreditation.

5. Applying Title IV regulations to institutions that do not seek participation in Title IV, but are accredited by Title IV-eligible institutions, has increased the cost of a college education. If an institution decides not to offer Title IV loans and Pell grants, that institution should not have to comply with Title IV regulations.

6. The publication of three-year default rates on student loans has revealed that too many colleges enroll students with no expectation that they will graduate. At present, a 30% default rate endangers an institution for loss of access to Title IV programs. That should be reduced to 20%. Any college or university with a three-year default rate greater than 20% should immediately be suspended for one year from access to Title IV programs.

7. Regional accreditation agencies that accredit only campus based institutions should not be permitted to accredit Internet programs offered by those institutions for one simple reason—they do not know enough about Internet instructional design and delivery.

8. Massive, open, online courses (MOOCs) offer a low-cost way to earn credits in introductory courses. At present the architecture of MOOCs is not compatible with Title IV regulations that require student engagement with instructors in discussion forums. Some States also require that authorized institutions offer courses with student/teacher engagement. The U.S. Department of Education should recognize an agency solely for the accreditation of MOOCs and adjust Title IV regulations to permit offering MOOCs for degree credit, if an institution offering MOOCs chooses not to participate in Title IV. If the Department fails to do that, Congress itself should charter such an agency. The Congress chartered Howard University, so there should be no objection to an accreditation agency chartered by Congress.

9. Shift a percentage of annual Title IV funding to the states in block grants and encourage the states to develop programs suited to market conditions in their states.

10. In order to qualify for these annual block grants, the States should be required to design programs that subsidize corporations that create training programs that guarantee employment for successful completion of that training.

11. Abolish NACIQI or reform its method of appointing members. Currently the membership of NACIQI consists of a disproportionate number of members appointed by the U.S. Department of Education. That number should be reduced to one and the balance assigned to the U.S. House and Senate in proportion to the number of Republican and Democrat members of Congress.

12. Abolish the U.S. Department of Education. Finally, let us agree that in a nation where education is the responsibility of the States, we do not need a "Ministry of Education." The U.S. Department of Education should be abolished and its programs assigned to other federal agencies or the States.

13. Organize education consumers for political action by forming a PAC. In order to achieve reform of American higher education, education consumers must participate in formation of Political Action Committees that make campaign contributions to federal elected officeholders. Milton Friedman was instrumental in developing a "school choice" organization that has been instrumental in establishing Voucher Programs in thirteen states. A federal PAC formed by education consumers can quickly gain a seat at the table where proposals for higher education reform are discussed by making donations to reform candidates. Higher education reform must become a topic of national discussion.

End Notes

1 "Rising Prices: College Tuition vs. the CPI," Center for College Affordability and Productivity, March 19, 2013.

2 http://www.ed.gov/news/press-releases/first-official-three-year-student-loan-default-rates-published

3 http://www2.ed.gov/offices/OSFAP/defaultmanagement/cdr.html

4 Visit http://www2.ed.gov/offices/OSFAP/defaultmanagement/cdr.html and count the number of colleges where one in every four students defaults on student loans.

5 An exception is Helen Dragas, a former rector of the University of Virginia, who attempted to reform UVA. She ultimately failed, but at least she tried. Susan Svrluga and Donna St. George, "Helen Dragas: The Leader who Forced out UVA's President." Washington Post, June 21, 2012.

6 Joseph Schumpeter, Capitalism, Socialism and Democracy, (New York: Harper and Brothers.1942).

7 The Institute for College Access & Success, College InSight: http://www.college-insight.org.

8 http://www.calstate.edu/budget/student-fees/fee-rates/systemwide-history.shtml

9 In the Winter 2017 session, California residents and non-residents are charged the same tuition cost.

10 Richard Bishirjian, "MOOCs vs. HCOCS," July 16, 2014: https://www.nas.org/articles/moocs_vs._hcocs_higher_cost_online_courses

11 http://www.calstate.edu/budget/student-fees/fee-rates/systemwide-history.shtml

12 Richard Bishirjian, "MOOCs vs. HCOCs."

13 Walter B. Wriston, *The Twilight of Sovereignty* (Bridgewater, NJ: Replica Books, 1997), 116–17.

14 Ibid., 115–16.

15 Ibid., 121.

16 Published by Simon and Schuster (Threshold Editions, 2010). This link takes you to a YouTube interview with Dr. Kurtz. https://www.youtube.com/watch?v=7IlGD2OABJE

17 Education Empire. David Brennan's White Hat Management, Inc. A Report by the Food and Allied Service Trades Division of the AFL-CIO in cooperation with the Ohio Federation of Teachers, 2006.

18 Richard Bishirjian, "The Creation of a Conservative Intellectual: 1960–65," in Modern Age, (Winter, 1998).

19 I'll Take My Stand: The South and the Agrarian Tradition (Baton Rouge, LSU Press, 2006). 75th Anniversary edition.

20 Patrick Burke, The Concept of Justice: Is Social Justice Just (London: Bloomsbury Studies in Political Philosophy, 2013).

21 See James Tunstead Burtchaell, The Dying of the Light: The Disengagement of Colleges and Universities from Their Christian Churches (Wm. B. Eerdmans Publishing Company, 1998).

22 Russell Nieli, From Christian Gentleman to Bewildered Seeker: The Transformation of American Higher Education. John William Pope Center for Higher Education Policy. (Raleigh, NC, 2007).

23 James Piereson, "The Left University," The Weekly Standard, October 3, 2005.

24 Peter Wood, Diversity: The Invention of a Concept (New York: Encounter Books, 2003).

25 Gates Notes, My Take on Technology & Teaching, March 1, 2011.

26 Carl Straumsheim, "Less Than 1%," InsideHigherEd.com, December 21, 2015.

27 Coursera, Udacity, Udemy.

28 Brown v. Board of Education of Topeka, 347 U.S. 483 (1954).

29 http://sheeo.org/sheeo_surveys

30 The City of Norfolk, Virginia made a $300,000 development grant to a "quality" restaurant in the Ocean View area of Norfolk to assure that it would remain in business. The owner of the restaurant later moved.

31 See Appendix C for an alphabetical list of states by total number of public employees.

32 Dr. Yecke was Associate Professor and Asst. Provost at Harding University in Searcy, Arkansas. Harding is affiliated with the Churches of Christ. Though Yecke served in a series of political appointed positions by Republican Governors, her actions demonstrated that Dr. Yecke knew nothing about the conservative movement and its commitment to limited government.

33 "Origins and End of the New World Order," Modern Age, (Summer 2004), pp. 195-209.

34 Benson, now President of the University of Colorado, has done little to advance conservative scholarship at CU and CU remains an important constituent of the Left University.

35 *A Guide to the H. B. Earhart Fellowship Program, 1952–2015,* ed. Cheryl Gorski (Ann Arbor, MI: The Trustees of Earhart Foundation, 2015).

36 The Republican-dominated government of North Carolina did not appreciate that Margaret Spellings is a big-government "educationist."

37 See Eric Voegelin, *Anamnesis,* trans. Gerhart Niemeyer (Columbia, MO: University of Missouri Press, 1990), page 193.

38 Doug Lederman, "Scrutiny for an Accreditor," InsideHigherEd.com, December 18, 2009.

39 Carl Straumsheim, "Feds Soften Distance Ed Rule," InsideHigherEd.com, July 25, 2016.

40 Christopher Finan, *From the Palmer Raids to the Patriot Act: A History of the Fight for Free Speech in America* (Boston, Beacon Press, 2007).

41 Ceased operations, April 26, 2015.

42 Kaplan, formerly owned by The Washington Post, is now owned by Graham Holdings.

43 Grand Canyon (LOPE) is expected to convert to not-for-profit status in order to avoid new regulations.

44 Daniel Bennett, "Crony Capitalism at the Department of Education," Minding the Campus, May 23, 2013.

45 Brody Mullins, "Former Education Official Faces Federal Investigation." Wall Street Journal, May 16, 2013.

46 Paul Fairn, "Accreditor on Life Support," InsideHigherEd.com, June 24, 2016.

47 The Mason Best Company was founded by Randy Best and Elvis Mason in 1984.

48 http://www.bestassociates.com

49 Milken Family Foundation "Education" statement at: http://www.mff.org/about-the-foundation/the- founders

50 http://sheeo.org/sheeo_surveys

Appedix A

MEMORANDUM

DATE: March 10, 2003
FROM: Richard J. Bishirjian, Ph.D.
TO: The Honorable Mark R. Warner
               The Honorable Jerry Kilgore
               Phyllis Palmiero, Executive Director, SCHEV
               Members of SCHEV's Council

RE: Proposed Certification Language: A Final Critique

I have had an opportunity to review revisions in proposed certification regulations and I am still convinced that their effect will be to freeze out the development of Internet education opportunities domiciled in the Commonwealth of Virginia.

Yorktown University, and, at most, three or four other proprietary education companies nationwide have utilized the Web to enter the education marketplace. In doing so, though they have no classrooms, no "sites" to be regulated, they are incorporated somewhere, and subject to regulations of their state of incorporation.

Only one such institution is domiciled in Virginia—Yorktown University. About Yorktown University there is no lack of information. Our founding investors are two not for-profit institutions whose Presidents live in Virginia: Paul Weyrich and Morton Blackwell. Our Chairman of the Board is a very prominent Fairfax, Virginia, attorney, Gilbert K. Davis.

And, the company began its existence by first incorporating in the Commonwealth, then applying for operating approval from SCHEV, and then by filing a registered security offer with the U.S. Securities and Exchange Commission. That offer was made effective by the State Corporation Commission of Virginia, and twenty-four other states.

Yorktown University recruited fifty distinguished faculty, many with former service in state and federal government, and we announced that we are "Putting Tradition Back into Education."

Still this digital technology and its uses for education are in the incubation stage, and formidable barriers exist to national and regional accreditation. Yorktown University may not expect to become nationally accredited until two and a half years after it enrolls its first student. And, because the regional accrediting association for this area (SACS) has never accredited a university that is solely based on the Internet, until those rules change, the only students Yorktown University may enroll who have some form of federal tuition assistance are members of our military services.

For that reason, we have developed two undergraduate degree programs, a MA in Government with concentrations in Political Economy and National Security Studies, and are developing an Executive MBA degree program, that will be marketed at tuition costs affordable to military personnel.

Regulations proposed by SCHEV will increase our costs, "bust" our budget, and destroy this business model. <u>Only an exemption of this University from proposed regulations will enable us to remain in the Commonwealth.</u>

I ask Council to consider seriously what it is proposing, and, perhaps, delay the imposition of new regulations until such time as their impact on this new industry has been fully analyzed.

Having made that request, I am providing you an analysis of SCHEV's revised proposed regulations to identify where they are in conflict with SCHEV's former practice, and with most other state regulations

Restrictions on the use of the name "University."
When Yorktown University first applied to SCHEV for operating authority, we were told that it couldn't use the name "University"

unless SCHEV granted approval. We have argued on several occasions that, if a new company desires to call itself a "University" in order to engage in financing its operations, it should be permitted to do so, as long as it doesn't enroll students using that name without SCHEV approval. I believe this provision is unconstitutional on its face, and constitutes a form of prior restraint on the fundamental, Constitutionally-protected freedom of speech.

The institution's catalog "shall clearly describe the institution's accreditation status."

"If the institution is not accredited, a statement regarding the status and timeframe for full accreditation" is required.
Two observations must be made about academic "accreditation." When Congress made regional accreditation the prerequisite for Title IV eligibility, it removed the six regional accrediting association's responsiveness to markets. As a result, a century-long decline in education quality accelerated, and regional accreditation no longer is a guarantee of "quality education," it merely guarantees access to $50 billion in annual tuition assistance.

"Accreditation" as that is currently assessed by all chartered accrediting associations, uses the "values clarification" method as the means to certify "quality." In other words, applicants are judged on the basis of having demonstrated that its constituents understand its "mission," and that the goals or values of that mission are achieved. The Values Clarification is a form of moral relativism that enables those assessed to see themselves in terms of their published goals or mission. <u>Accreditation does not reflect a consensus about what constitutes a good and happy life.</u> There is no such consensus in Academe today, which is why, in the past fifteen years, an ideology called "political correctness" has come to dominate the "value systems" of our universities.

Though SCHEV has responsibility for higher education in the Commonwealth, nothing in SCHEV's regulations addresses the closure of our academic institutions to the quest for truth, closure to knowledge and understanding about Western civilization, closure to the Judeo-Christian tradition, nor even closure to the history of the Commonwealth of Virginia. In focusing on new, proposed, regulations that touch on "process," not educational content, SCHEV has abdicated the moral high ground, and proposes to fill the Code of Virginia with regulations distrustful of proprietary education companies that do business in the state, and the students who willingly enroll as degree candidates because the proprietary sector is the most innovative, progressive, force in education today.

Requiring that non-accredited institutions state that they are not accredited reflects SCHEV's lack of understanding of the cultural collapse of higher education standards, and the role accreditation has played in fostering that collapse.

Attached to this message is February 11, 2003 letter to Members of Congress by Cong. Thomas Petri titled "Is Accreditation Necessary." Cong. Petri, and a coalition of Members of Congress, are well aware that "accreditation" is of no educational value, and they are moving to de-couple accreditation as the criterion for Title IV eligibility.

If the Higher Education Act reauthorization decouples Title IV eligibility from regional accreditation, hundreds of institutions will no longer aspire to regional accreditation, but will become eligible on the basis of audited financial statements submitted to the U.S. Department of Education.

Must these institutions then say that they have not met the standard of full accreditation?

In essence what I am arguing is that SCHEV represents a philosophy of control, regulation, and a distaste for competition, free markets, and the free choice of citizens enjoying the benefits of markets. And it manifests that animosity at the very moment that, at the federal level, we may see some relaxation in regulation of education and control.

Annual Recertification.

SCHEV seeks to require that existing institutions "re-certify" annually. In all honesty, recertification would be a) a nightmare of the first order for those institutions regulated by SCHEV, b) a dangerous Sword of Damocles for stock corporations, especially those publicly traded, and with operating approval solely in the

Commonwealth, AND c) would compel an order-of-magnitude upward revision in this institution's budget. We calculate that the minimum cost of recertification for Yorktown University is an annual regulatory tax of $35,000.

This proposed regulation, on its face, achieves two things:

a) That every institution operating in the Commonwealth is at risk annually of losing its "license," and

b) That SCHEV will increase its staff to monitor re-certification documents.

The first imposes a regulatory burden (in effect a tax) on existing companies that will compel "stock" companies to leave the Commonwealth because even the possibility of a loss of license will drive investors away; and the second assures that SCHEV will grow its staff. Our securities markets haven't recovered from the meltdown of high tech stocks, yet Virginia expects stock companies to remain domiciled here, even though they may lose their license to operate at any moment. Here is another reason to grant an exemption to the only Internet-based university operating in the Commonwealth.

Though SCHEV's executive director may argue that SCHEV only has twenty-five staff, I believe a close analysis of other states will show that this staff complement represents a bloated bureaucracy that could, easily, be reduced by half, if some of the more crippling powers Gordon Davies gave to SCHEV in his twenty-five-year career of empire-building were removed.

Recertification surely compels an exponential increase in staff so designated. In a recession, when all other agencies of government are facing reductions in force, SCHEV demonstrates a compelling need to grow staff.

Annual Fees

Originally, SCHEV proposed an annual fee of $10,000 for the five un-accredited institutions operating in the state. That has been reduced to $5,000, but accredited institutions only pay a fee of $2,300. This is, on its face, offensive.

Instead of assessing certified institutions an annual fee, how about reducing SCHEV's staff by the amount of new fees?

Or, why not assess <u>every</u> institution in the state the same annual fee?

"General Education courses"

Currently, SCHEV requires that only state universities require students to take thirty semester hours in General Education subjects "in each of the following areas; the humanities/fine arts, the social/behavioral sciences, and the natural sciences/mathematics. The curriculum must provide components designed to ensure competence in reading, writing, oral communication, fundamental mathematical skills, and the basic use of computers." DETC accreditation requires thirty semester hours in General Education subjects, but does not direct institutional members to specify exactly what general education courses are to be taken.

SCHEV's original Draft Certification Language proposed to apply state university general education standards to private universities. My concern is that, in this one area where I approve of what SCHEV proposes, it has not gone far enough.

SCHEV's current core General Education requirements are not academically sound. They do not require students at state universities to take courses in American Government, the history of The Commonwealth of Virginia; principles of Economics, religious studies, English literature. Nor is there a requirement that every student at a state university take two semester courses in the History of Western Civilization. If SCHEV were more interested in academic matters, all education in the Commonwealth would benefit.

All instructional courses for degree credit ... require 15 class contact hours (45 hours total for a three-credit course).

This requirement, not a new requirement but re-stated in the Draft Certification Language document, exceeds the federal standard.

The *Chronicle of Higher Education*, September 6, 2002, page A43, reports that the U.S. Department of Education has changed the requirement that "college programs that don't operate on a traditional academic calendar to deliver at least 12 hours of course work a week for their students to be eligible to receive federal financial aid." This rule has been dropped, allowing distance learning institutions more flexibility in designing curricula.

The Chronicle reports, "With both the 12-hour and 50-percent rules relaxed, 'you would see a real move toward distance and online education...'"

Virginia, through SCHEV, maintains a standard more severe than the federal government, and does not take into consideration the difference between distance and traditional education.

This is only one of several instances in which the Draft Certification Language <u>does not</u> account for the differences between Internet-based and classroom instruction. For example,

SCHEV states that "each institution shall provide students ... a catalog, bulletin or brochure..."
Yorktown University is solely Internet-based and every document it generates is available online, not in printed "catalog, bulletin or brochure" form. The language SCHEV uses reflects traditional practices, not those engendered by new technologies, and could be interpreted to mean that this institution should incur expensive print publication costs not suitable for an Internet-based company.

"The institution's refund policy" should state that the "Institution only accepts tuition on a per-term/services rendered disbursement basis."
Here, too, the traditional concept of "term" is employed that does not adapt to the ways of Internet institutions. And, what does a regulation of this specificity have to do with SCHEV's fundamental charter? What next will SCHEV require? Restrictions on which credit cards we are allowed to accept?

Most Internet colleges operate on an Open Admission basis, or Directed Reading schedule AND/OR a schedule of five ten-week terms, or sometimes six eight-week "terms." It is not practical (nor even meaningful) when dealing with students eligible for DANTES or Title IV funds to restrict tuition policy to one out of five or six terms a year. SCHEV's regulation regarding "tuition per term" could kill an institution that requires degree candidates to take three courses a year to maintain their degree candidacy.

Again, SCHEV is thinking (and its language reflects) traditional practices, not the reality of Internet education.

Annual audits or financial reviews

Because Yorktown University operates as efficiently as it can, and is not obliged to conduct costly financial audits by DETC, it has not maintained audited financial information of its first two full years of operation. It does retain the services of a Certified Public Accountant. The cost of audits can easily be $10,000 annually. For startup Internet universities the audit or financial review requirement proposed here should be waived, and submission of tax returns by Certified Financial Accountants substituted.

The institution shall maintain a surety bond ... adequate to provide refunds to students for the unused portion of tuition and fees for any given semester, quarter, or term.

In a review by Yorktown University staff of regulations of other states, we could not find a state with as severe a Surety Bond standard as proposed by SCHEV. Ten percent to twenty percent of the refund due students is standard, not 100%.

Not many years ago, the Commonwealth of Virginia was fondly referred to as the "Digital Dominion." SCHEV's regulations are not in keeping with the promise of that vision, nor the promise of the digital revolution in education that can transform the delivery of educational products to Virginia's consumers. A small traditional college that is just beginning its existence, may easily require $30 million in order to assure its survival. Digital technologies make it possible for Internet colleges to commence operations, and achieve positive cash flow, delivering courses and degree programs on the Web with assets of far less than $1 million.

That reality, and anticipated de-regulation by the 108th Congress, could make the Digital Dominion a reality for hundreds of new colleges and universities exploiting the web.

Please let me be clear here. What is at stake is not simply competition with the education market in Virginia. The world made available to us all by the Internet is national and in fact global. SCHEV is not just driving out of Virginia businesses with statewide markets. It's making it undesirable and, perhaps, impossible to base global businesses here.

If new Certification Language is adopted, Virginia will become the Appalachia of digitally delivered higher education.

The impact of this provision on universities that are solely Internet-based is disproportionate to the impact on established, traditional, classroom institutions. Again, the industry we represent is in the incubation stage, and the Surety Bond requirement will drive Yorktown University from the state.

The positive development of the digital, new economy will not occur in Virginia if SCHEV imposes these financial requirements and maintains its policy of "top down" bureaucratic administration of the education marketplace.

Whenever Yorktown University advertises employment opportunities, we are inundated by applications from residents of Hampton Roads with excellent credentials employed in occupations far below their level of education. Recently, American Military University left the Commonwealth to reside in West Virginia. Though its reasons were motivated by regional accrediting regulations, I'm confident that SCHEV regulations were also a consideration. At a time in the local, state and national economy when less regulation is called for, SCHEV asks for "Emergency" authority. I fear that a "disconnect" exists between the offices of SCHEV in the James Madison Building in Richmond, and the local, state, and national mood.

Who Must Comply?

Lastly, I would like to ask some questions that, on their face, new regulatory proposals do not answer, and I request an answer before the next meeting of SCHEV's Council on March 19.

Why are these regulations being proposed?

Having read original and proposed regulations, I am not certain that the certified education community in the Commonwealth understands to whom new regulations apply. If an institution is certified in the state, but is not incorporated here, must it comply with new regulations?

If an institution is incorporated here, but has no classrooms, must it comply with new regulations?

If an institution is not certified here, may it engage in advertising its educational products in the Commonwealth?

And lastly I must ask the following question:

"Can Virginia Afford SCHEV?"

The above questions touch on the highly technical nature of the *Empire of Codes* developed by SCHEV's former Executive Director Gordon Davies, and which inflicts injury on all institutions operating on the state, and increases of the cost of higher education for Virginia's students.

The "Empire of Codes" is so technical that new institutions (foolish enough to incorporate here) may easily incur, in addition to the newly proposed $50,000 Surety Bond, costs similar to what we incurred in 2000. Applying for certification easily cost Yorktown University $35,000. And that was before SCHEV proposed an annual fee. The president of Patrick Henry College told me he incurred costs in excess of $100,000.

I think one single question should be asked by members of the General Assembly and the Governor of the Commonwealth: "Can the Commonwealth of Virginia afford, in its present form, a regulatory body like SCHEV?"

Sincerely yours,
Richard J. Bishirjian, Ph.D. President

Appendix B

Robert Shireman, Deputy Undersecretary of Education
Speech to The National Association of State Administrators
and Supervisors of Private School
April 28 2010

Two and a half or three years ago, we started to see a serious economic slide downward in this country; credit markets had seized up, the sub-prime mortgage issue was a major cause of that and we started seeing people losing their jobs. We saw people in their jobs feeling much more insecure, much less secure about their ability to invest in higher education, their ability to buy a home with the collapse of the credit markets, and the way to solve that—long-term—is to invest in improving our nation's economy, to invest in the kind of innovation that comes from education, the productivity increases that come from job training.

In order to follow up on that, President Obama laid out a bold goal for the country. He said that by 2020, we want to regain our place as the number one country in the world in terms of adults with postsecondary credentials, college degrees, certificates and other job training programs. In the recovery legislation, now about a year and a half ago, that included an expansion of the tax credits that [x] hoping to create in the 90s, an expansion of that tax credit to $2500, making it for four years and actually covering more of the types of expenses that students and families have for higher education. Increases in Pell Grants—the usual approach and what you have seen in your own states—are in an econ downturn; more people are poor, more people want to go to school, but instead of following up on that need by putting more money into the grant and scholarship programs, actually less money goes into the grant and scholarship programs because of the state budgets.

Federal government took the opposite approach really: what needs to be countercyclical spending that helps—like unemployment insurance; spending that needs to follow up on and help to address the new gaps that families are seeing.

The tax credits were part of that. The increases in Pell Grants are not only meeting the new demand for Pell Grant dollars, but actually increasing the size of the Pell Grants and proving those increases into the future with the follow-up legislation passed a few weeks ago—also restoring some certainty to the student loan program, and making sure that no one has any reason to doubt whether they will be able to get the federal student loans that they need.

I mentioned that when people are losing their jobs, when people become insecure in their jobs, they look for higher education; they look to find what kind of job training can I get, what kind of skills can I add to my repertoire, what are the skills that I have, how can I make them better so that I'll keep my job, or if I lose my job I'll have options. And at the same time, while we saw this increase in demand, which is helpful and useful given what the President had to say about the need to train our population, we saw state tax revenue declining in all but a few states; we saw cuts in the budgets of state colleges and universities and community colleges, resulting in a combination of very large increases in tuition in some cases and reduced enrollments, fewer seats. So increased demand—people wanting more education and training—and public institutions either had fewer seats and were charging more tuition, or might not declare they were going to be enrolling fewer people but their course offerings are cut—the result is they are not able to meet the demand for higher education.

Tuition-driven institutions didn't react that way because they're tuition-driven institutions, and the nonprofit institutions have done pretty well despite significant declines in their endowments because there continued to be significant demand for higher education.

The nonprofit private colleges did well, and, in particular, the for-profit institutions have come in with investors making sure that there was capacity to be able to serve additional students.

They knew that those students would come with those federal dollars—Pell Grants, student loans, tax credits—and that that would help them to not only be consumers who want higher ed, but consumers who can pay for that higher education with that federal support, so the for-profit industry, more than any other in these economic difficult times, has responded.

I want to give you some specific numbers. We now post on one of the [X] Web sites, the quarterly numbers of Pell Grants by different kinds of schools, so I looked at what the first 3 quarters – the total of the first 3 quarters of this award year compared to the last award year for some of the schools that I knew would be here today. For example:

Corinthian Colleges – 38% increase for first three quarters this year compared to last year for a total of $800M

DeVry – a couple people here from DeVry? – 42% increase up to $1.7B

ITT – you guys here? A 44% increase up to $623M

Strayer – still here? Is that you? Well this one – 95% increase, maybe something about the quarters, but up to $414M

APEI – Wally here? And Russell? 94% increase up to $44M

Kaplan – they here? This total is actually all the Washington Post-owned entities; 33% increase up to $909M; and, again, this is the first 3 quarters of the year, so the totals for the year are obviously more than that

Career Education Corporation – 29% increase up to $1B this first three quarters

EDMC – several folks here; a 16% increase, $1.1B

Capella – over there? 40% increase to $378M

And I think I've just got a couple of others:

Grand Canyon – 55% increase to $260M

University of Phoenix – you there? – 9% increase, but obviously that's on a larger base. Probably that increase is as much as a lot of others' total dollars, and that increase is $2.7B total

And Bridgepoint – you guys here? – 61% increase, $393M

I think those were all that I had numbers for; obviously I know that there are a few others here as well.

So I wanted to begin just by thanking the for-profit industry for responding to the critical demands from people out there who need higher education. I'd like everybody to give them a hand.

Now, others of us in the room have the responsibility for making sure those federal funds I just listed—for education and training—that it's all totally above board. That those significant increases in federal spending for higher education—loans, grants—are serving students and taxpayers as well as they possibly can. That is what the Triad is about, and I know I can say triad in front of this audience because I heard somebody say it earlier. I want to talk for a second about some things going on in Washington right now, and I don't mean negotiated rulemaking. I will get to that in a few minutes, but there is a Wall Street reform debate going on right now in Washington.

What happened in that credit crisis a couple of years ago had something to do with credit rating agencies – agencies like S&P, Fitch, other agencies that were responsible for rating instruments – financial instruments, looking at what is the quality of these things that have names that cause people's eyes to roll over – things like collateralized debt obligations, and other kinds of securitizations. So what is the quality of the loans, mortgages? Are they going to be repaid? How likely are these loans to be repaid so that an investor purchasing this…how confident can they be that when they purchase, when they invest in this particular instrument, that they will get the money back that they are expecting?

The business model for these rating agencies has come under fire in these meetings in Washington; part of this has to do with the business model of the rating agencies—on the one hand, their responsibility, their job, the core of their business was to make sure they did a good job providing an honest rating for the instrument that they were analyzing. On the other hand, they relied on the income from the companies who asked them to rate the instrument, and I'll read to you from – a NY Times – some of the emails that have been coming out recently.

In 2004, well before Wall Street's bets on sub-prime mortgages became widely known, employees at Standard & Poor's credit rating agency were feeling pressure to expand the business. One employee warned in an internal email that the company would lose business if it failed to give high enough ratings to collateralized debt obligations, the investments that later emerged at the heart of the financial crisis.

Quote: "We are meeting with your group this week to discuss adjusting criteria for rating CDOs of real estate assets because of the ongoing threat of losing deals. Lose the CDO and lose the base business. A self-reinforcing loop."

In other words, if we don't loosen up in our assessment of these instruments, nobody is going to come have their instruments assessed by us anymore. And this created a conflict which led to instruments that should have been questioned not being questioned, and [leading] over to the financial crisis that we have been suffering from for the past couple of years.

The other issue besides the business model was the complexity and fast growth of different kinds of instruments and I'll read from another of the recent articles. "Email documents and other messages suggested that executives and analysts at ratings agencies embraced new business from Wall Street even though they recognized that they couldn't properly analyze all of the banks' products." And one of the other quotes ends with, "we were so overwhelmed."

So I want to actually ask, on that issue—the complexity and growth—and I know we're feeling this with publicly traded corporations and purchases going this way and that way, and we're trying to figure out what's going on. Are there regulators in the room who feel like you DO have the analytical firepower you need to assess what is going on with the entities you regulate in higher education? Those who do feel you have the firepower you need? I don't think we feel we have the firepower we need.

So with the reform on the financial instrument side of the equation, and what they're really talking about now in Washington on financial reform, one analyst—an academic looking at what's going on—said it only tinkers with the workings of the ratings agency; it doesn't end the inherent conflicts of interest, those conflicts of interest where the people who do the rating are paid for by those who do the ratings. This whole situation with credit agencies, credit rating agencies, is, as I see it, very similar to the way accrediting agencies work in this country—the same kind of inherent conflict of interest. Albeit accrediting agencies are nonprofit, and on top of that, what would this crisis look like if the banks had actually been the ones running the credit agencies and were doing a peer review kind of model, which is the model we have in accreditation, where it is the regulated who are really looking at each other rather than an outside entity?

So to borrow from Winston Churchill, accreditation, as a part of that triad, in terms of a way of assessing quality in higher education, is the worst form of accountability except for all of the others. What Winston Churchill actually said was, democracy is the worst form of government, except for all the others. So I am bringing up this issue of accreditation not to say that we should back away from it or change it; I actually don't have a better system for us for assessing quality in higher education. But it is problematic, and we need to remember that as the other two pieces of the triad—as we figure out how we can do the best job possible in our responsibilities. Federal and state governments cannot rely on accreditation to ensure that consumers and taxpayers are protected to the full extent that they need to be. All three legs of that three-legged stool need to be working and working well.

There are a number of things that we're doing, you've heard about some of them – elevating, monitoring and enforcement. We're working with the inspector general at the Department of Education, taking a much closer look at data than ever before to help guide our selection for program reviews and investigations when necessary by the inspector general, working with the Federal Trade Commission to join their consumer complaint system so complaints they get and other agencies that are on their consumer sentinel; working on the issue of how we can look more at issues of misrepresentation as we do program reviews and other kinds of monitoring.

A second area besides the monitoring and enforcement is improving consumer information. We have put graduation rates, retention rates and transfer rates right on the FAFSA form when students are choosing colleges. The rates are right there as a reminder to students that they should do some good shopping, look at various kinds of data that might help them to compare schools. We're also providing them with a more detailed financial aid estimate in terms of the financial aid that they can get, and this is partly to make sure that people know they can get that aid wherever they go. Sometimes students think, oh I can get that $12K because the school costs $12K, and I would only get $3K at a community college that only cost $3K—not realizing that, in fact, if they wanted to get more than what tuition costs at that community college so that they can focus on their studies instead of working excessive hours, that that is something that they can have available to them.

And starting this summer, as a result of a regulatory process that was already completed, schools will have to begin providing placement information, and where they have placement rates, they actually will need to make students aware on their Web sites of placement rates they have for programs that they are offering.

Uh, coordination and sharing—I headed some of the discussion in prior sessions and I look forward to this afternoon's discussion. Within the federal government, we are working with the Federal Trade Commission, the Veterans Administration around the GI Bill, the SEC because of the involvement of publicly traded institutions, and states...we have encouraged involvement in this group and are looking for other ways that we can help. Happy to discuss that in Q&A here as well as this afternoon, because we really need to become good partners if we're going to do best by taxpayers and students.

And accreditors, there are some new requirements; we're working on sharing some draft guidance related to all of the requirements for accreditors, and again building that triad and all working together. In fact, I was actually on the Internet looking for a three- legged stool to see if I could bring one for this, and I noticed one of the three-legged stools had not only the three legs, but it had this connecting piece of wood that held the three legs together. I thought, well that would be the perfect prop, because that would demonstrate it's a strong stool if that connector is there, making it as strong as possible.

Also, many of you have heard, reviewing the rules and regulations and where appropriate revising, in the process of revising those rules. Let me take a little bit of time to tell you about some of those. We started about a year ago, doing public hearings where we basically said, we want to know whether we need to improve program integrity—are there things we need to be doing? Here's a list of some areas: misrepresentation, definition of credit hour, state authorization, other kinds of things, and we saw input. We did three public hearings. People were able to submit items over the Internet, through email, and we got a lot of input about great schools out there— students who were having a good experience, people who attended the schools, got a job, had a great experience. We also heard from former students who felt that they were misled, and legal aid attorneys who had clients whose stories were cause for concern.

That was followed up by – we asked for nominations for people to serve on committees. The way this whole process works is that we do our best to work through possible rule changes with a committee of stakeholders, recommended, nominated by interested parties, states, various institutions, student organizations, legal aid. For three week-long sessions, December, January and February, we went through each of 14 issues talking about changes that might make sense.

One of them is misrepresentation—clarification really against misrepresentation by schools.

High school diploma – one of those things that you take to somebody and think, how hard can it be to know if a high school diploma is valid? As you know, not that easy and many of you are at the state level, so you know that the state isn't necessarily declaring who is good or bad. And the issue of the federal government declaring what is a valid HS education, for example, gets into areas where the federal government isn't supposed to be declaring such things, so a more complicated issue than I think a lot of people expected. We are making – at least in neg-reg session – reached some tentative agreement around the definition.

I would say the most significant thing we are doing is looking at – and I think this is now a likelihood – when people apply on the FAFSA and it asks for a HS diploma, a list will actually pop up and they can enter what that high school is, the name of that high school, based on some federal lists we have. It won't necessarily mean that it will be a valid high school, but it does give us and you the ability to, if, for example, it's a suspected diploma mill, we would be able to see who are, and where are the students going who are using this particular high school as the place they say they got their diploma from. And if we find that it's some particular colleges, that means that it might be encouraging people to go and use a diploma mill. So it will be a useful tool for us and you as well, and that's the most important change we'll be making there.

Incentive compensation was a major issue—the issue of paid recruiters. A number of years ago, a number of safe harbors were created and there was a lot of indication that they were wider loopholes than are appropriate, given the wording of the actual law that prohibits payment of actual compensation based on enrollment. So that's another one that we are working on.

State authorization – I heard California mentioned and it was a surprise to me when I came to Washington and asked about California to discover a legal interpretation of the Dept. of Ed. – well, if the school is not authorized, then it is authorized. So this raised a question that came up in neg-reg about what is at least some minimum standard about what kind of authorization should count in terms of the state role in that Triad.

Satisfactory academic progress is another area taking attendance. What I used to call R2D2, return to Title IV. I'm not mentioning all of the issues, but the final one I will talk some about is Gainful Employment, and this is the one that's been in the news a lot. It seems that every time I speak somewhere, someone thinks I said something new and calls a stock analyst who then reports it, causing the stocks to go up or down or whatever, and I assure you I am not going to say anything new. If you are a stock analyst or you know a stock analyst, the answer when they ask you, "What did Shireman say?" you say nothing new.

So the statute—the federal law—requires that in order for some programs to be eligible for federal financial aid, they have to lead to gainful employment in a recognized occupation. This applies to non-degree programs at any type of school and it applies to most programs at for-profit schools; really all except some BA, liberal arts programs through an exception—a recently enacted exception—that actually begins this July 1st. But for the most part, a for-profit institution, in order to be eligible for federal financial aid, has to show that the program leads to gainful employment or prepares the student for gainful employment in a recognized occupation.

So a year ago, we began asking the question: what is the definition, what should be the definition of gainful employment in a recognized occupation? We had hoped that perhaps some schools would come forward and say, "Well when we start a program, here's how we determine whether or not it complies." We didn't get that kind of information.

We brought it up in neg-reg and made some suggestions for discussion. We suggested maybe there should be some relationship to the debt levels that students are taking on and the expected earnings that they may have from the occupations that you have identified that you are preparing people for. We also suggested that perhaps a loan repayment rate approach could be devised where we would be able to see that federal loans are actually being repaid at a rate that makes sense if people were actually gainfully employed.

We looked at the provision and current regulation that currently applies to very short programs—the 70/70 rule—70 percent completion rate, 70 percent placement rate, and asked: should something like that be part of the definition of gainful employment? And then for new programs, we suggested maybe there should be something from an employer, who employs people in the occupations that the program is preparing people for, that at least asserts that yes, the curriculum, the program that I've seen at this school is designed in a way where it would prepare people for the jobs that I have in my particular business. So, we suggested that for new programs.

Now, in every other issue in neg-reg, we got pretty good discussion at the table. Sometimes we actually got consensus from the group on what we should actually, how regulation should actually be worked out. But for some reason, on the gainful employment issue, we didn't get the kind of discussion that would at least help to guide in a very constructive way, the direction, and to know, well, this would be okay with certain kinds of schools, but wouldn't be okay with other kinds of schools.

Instead, the reaction from, in particular, those who were representing the for-profit colleges was—you can't do this, you can't define this term, why are you doing this? — and that continued even after the neg-reg sessions. We continued to meet; we have gotten improved input, improved feedback. And where things stand now with whole regulatory packed—so everything I've just discussed now including the gainful employment—is that in the next few weeks there will be proposed rule published in the *Federal Register*. There will be a comment period after that proposed rule is published. That will be the appropriate time to suggest changes or express support for provisions, suggest alternatives, and then a final rule. Our goal would be to publish a final rule by November 1st. For rules to take effect, in general, next year from this July, they need to be published by November 1st. So that's where we will be; that's the timeline for the rule going forward.

I wanted to conclude my remarks before going to some Q&A and some discussion with a piece that Thomas Frank wrote in the *WSJ*. The title of the article is, "Obama and the Regulatory Capture," and it is, again, back about the financial regulation:

"It was not merely structural problems that led certain regulators to nap through the crisis. The people who filled regulatory jobs in the past Administration were asleep at the switch because they were supposed to be. It was as though they had been hired for their extraordinary powers of drowsiness. The reason for that is simple: There are powerful institutions that don't like being regulated. Regulation sometimes cuts into their profits and interferes with their business. So they have used the political process to sabotage, redirect, defund, undo or hijack the regulatory state since the regulatory state was first invented."

So, he follows that up with one more line here:

"And it created a situation where banking regulators posed for pictures with banking lobbyists while putting a chainsaw to a pile of regulations. Smiles all around. Let the fellows at IndyMac do whatever they want."

So my closing word is, we should take the photos, we should smile, but let's not shirk our responsibility for regulating the industry. The schools will make plenty of money and students and taxpayers will be better off if we do our jobs as best as we can. Thank you very much.

———————————

Unedited Transcript. © 2010 *Career Education Review*. Michael J. Cooney, editor

Appendix C

Public Employees by State (2014)

STATE GOVERNMENT: EMPLOYMENT AND PAYROLL DATA BY STATE AND BY FUNCTION: MARCH 2014

State	Public Employees
AL Total	78,120
AK Total	25,068
AZ Total	65,846
AR Total	57,095
CA Total	333,083
CO Total	57,780
CT Total	53,662
DE Total	23,249
FL Total	159,008
GA Total	116,251
HI Total	52,434
ID Total	20,270
IL Total	102,078
IN Total	74,507
IA Total	40,053
KS Total	44,041
KY Total	74,615
LA Total	68,801
ME Total	18,602
MD Total	78,023
MA Total	88,601

MI Total	113,140
MN Total	68,042
MS Total	51,670
MO Total	78,298
MT Total	16,877
NE Total	26,733
NV Total	24,524
NH Total	14,694
NJ Total	130,261
NM Total	41,263
NY Total	222,965
NC Total	126,735
ND Total	15,747
OH Total	109,085
OK Total	88,527
OR Total	57,826
PA Total	140,760
RI Total	17,073
SC Total	70,754
SD Total	12,774
TN Total	70,425
TX Total	278,324
UT Total	46,059
VA Total	107,885
WA Total	99,079
WV Total	36,579
WI Total	58,052
WY Total	12,361

SOURCE: 2014 Annual Survey of Public Employment & Payroll. http://www.census.gov/govs/apes/how_data_collected.html

Appendix D

Users and Performers
act adopt anticipate apply calculate demonstrate execute help operate perform show use utilize

Problem Finders and Solvers
analyze anticipate argue criticize derive discover evaluate examine explore inquire hypothesize investigate predict prioritize question resolve search solve survey verify

Creators and Producers
cause compose construct create design develop devise establish evoke fashion formulate implement inaugurate initiate innovate institute invent make modify organize plan produce propose revise

Students and Thinkers
assess categorize classify compare contrast critique decipher deduce define describe detect diagnose differentiate estimate evaluate explain extend generalize hypothesize infer interpret judge justify order outline predict prioritize rank recommend solve summarize validate

Listeners and Communicators
acknowledge argue clarify comprehend correspond demonstrate depict describe discuss elaborate exhibit explain express imitate indicate paraphrase persuade portray recite recount relate respond restate show speak state write

Teachers and Mentors
advise anticipate assist coach counsel demonstrate educate

empathize encourage expect explain guide impart mentor model negotiate nurture resolve show suggest

Team Members and Partners
accept accommodate agree allow assist collaborate connect contribute cooperate defend demand encourage facilitate help offer persuade praise protect recognize resolve share support unite

Leaders and Organizers
anticipate arrange coordinate decide direct empower encourage endure engage enlist ensure establish facilitate formulate harmonize implement initiate inspire intervene lead manage mesh organize persist plan praise preserve supervise support systemize

Appendix E

About the Author

Richard J. Bishirjian, Ph.D. is a businessman and educator. He earned a B.A. from the University of Pittsburgh and a Ph.D. in Government and International Studies from the University of Notre Dame under the direction of Gerhart Niemeyer. While at Notre Dame he studied under Eric Voegelin, Stanley Parry, Henri Deku and Ralph McInerny. He did advanced study with Michael Oakeshott at the London School of Economics and studied Sanskrit at the Southern Asia Institute, Columbia University, classical Greek at Hunter College and Latin at Loyola University of Chicago.

Dr. Bishirjian taught at universities and colleges in Indiana, Texas and New York. He is the author of a history of political theory, editor of A Public Philosophy Reader that was cited by the Intercollegiate Studies Institute as one of the best studies of conservatism. In 2015 St. Augustine's Press published Dr. Bishirjian's The Conservative Rebellion.

Appointed to Ronald Reagan's Office of the President-Elect, he served as a team leader with responsibility for the National Endowment for the Humanities, and was appointed by President Reagan as Acting Associate Director of the United States International Communication Agency, formerly USIA. He served on the staff of the United States Senate. He was president and founder of World News Institute, and Associate Director of Boston University, College of Communication.

Beginning with the fall of the Berlin wall, he worked in East and Central Europe as a privatization consultant or in partnerships with major corporations. He later served as privatization consultant to the County of Allegheny, Pittsburgh, Pennsylvania.

Dr. Bishirjian has been a member of the Philadelphia Society since 1975 and served for many years as an Editorial Advisor to the quarterly journal, founded by Russell Kirk, Modern Age.